To Cox
From - Dad & Mom
1986

To Cox
From - Dad & Mom
1986

Hockey!

The World of the Pros

Hockey!
The World of the Pros

Michael A. Berger
Photography by Bruce Bennett

NEW YORK

First published in USA 1986
by Exeter Books
Distributed by Bookthrift
Exeter is a trademark of Bookthrift Marketing, Inc.
Bookthrift is a registered trademark of Bookthrift Marketing, Inc.
New York, New York

ISBN 0-671-08342-2

This book was designed and produced by
Footnote Productions Ltd.
4/6 Blundell Street
London N7 9BH

Composition by Best-set Typesetter Ltd., Hong Kong.
Color origination by Regent Publishing Services Ltd.
Printed by Lee-Fung Asco Printers Ltd.

Editorial Director: Sheila Buff
Art Director: Ken Diamond, Art Patrol/NYC

Printed in Hong Kong.

Contents

Acknowledgments

Thank yous are difficult things to issue: too few and people are insulted; too many and the gesture means nothing. But here goes:

Thanks to Sheila Buff and Tony Meisel at Footnote Productions for their confidence in handing me this project sight unseen (me, that is), especially with so tight a deadline on their end. And thanks to Bruce Bennett for having the confidence to recommend me for the book. Further thanks to Bruce and also to Brian Winkler and Lindsay Silverman for their outstanding photos.

Thanks to the players, coaches, managers and announcers quoted in this book for their time and patience, given under sometimes trying circumstances.

Special thanks to National Hockey League linesman Gordie Broseker for one of the most enlightening lunches I've ever had.

Finally, thanks to the NHL for giving me something to do on my nights off. Enjoy.

To those who've always helped: Paul, Bruce and Robert J; Stan and Rich; and of course, my three biggest fans — Mom, Dad and Eric.

Hockey isn't called the world's fastest game for nothing. The grace, artistry and yes, brutality, all clash at a dizzying speed to form a dramatic spectacle.

Many times what occurs on the ice does so at such speed that even the most knowledgeable fan is unaware of what he has seen. This book is an attempt — in words and pictures — to take you a little closer, to give you a better look. Players, coaches and other NHL personnel will explain, in their own words, the whos, whys and whats of the game today. You'll get an inside look at the components that give hockey its excitement and drama.

All you have to do is turn the pages.

Centres

Mario Lemieux topped the 100-point mark for the second straight time in 1985–86, posting 141 points and finishing second to Edmonton's Wayne Gretzky in league scoring.

No position, throughout the history of the National Hockey League, has ever been a more glamourous one than that of centre. Other positions on the ice may have been home to the more explosive exploits of a right wing like Maurice "The Rocket" Richard, or the dynamics of a defenceman like Bobby Orr, but centres have long been the stars, the point around which every other position has rotated.

It was no accident, for example, that when the Montreal Canadiens bought an entire junior hockey league it was to secure the services of Jean Beliveau, one of the most graceful players ever to lace on skates.

Beliveau was, of course, a centre.

In today's game, centres come in all shapes and sizes. Some blend solid offensive skills with an effective defencive game, while others shine with particular skills of either the offensive or defencive variety.

One of the league's outstanding young centres brings back memories of Beliveau, with his artistic skating, magnificent puck-handling abilities and offensive skills. Not surprisingly, the youngster is French-Canadian and, to complete the Beliveau comparison, was a much-sought-after prize in the NHL's Entry Draft.

Mario Lemieux, Pittsburgh's super centre, established himself as a force to be reckoned with in his freshman NHL campaign, when he tallied 100 points for what was then a woeful Penguins team. He made a 40-goal scorer out of 29-year-old journeyman winger Warren Young, also an NHL freshman during the 1984–85 season.

So confident were the Penguins of the impact that Lemiuex would have on the team that they featured him in all their season-ticket mailings and promotions. Even a summer of sometimes bitter contract negociations couldn't dampen Lemieux's effect in Steel City. Before he ever set stick to puck, Mario Lemieux was The Franchise in Pittsburgh.

Throughout the 1983–84 season, the Penguins coveted Lemieux while he was collecting 282 points in 70 junior games with the Laval Voisins of the Quebec Major Junior Hockey League. They made no secret of their plans to draft him and make him the foundation of their team.

That expectation could create terrible problems even for a veteran, so imagine what could have happened to Lemieux. But Pittsburgh's general manager, Eddie Johnston, couldn't be happier.

"Mario's done everything we've asked and he's done things we haven't asked him to do, too," says Johnston.

As if to disavow the lengthy contract negociations that preceded his arrival in Pittsburgh — and to prove his heart really was in the Steel City — Lemieux arrived at his first training camp a week early. He became the first player to slap a goalie's pads after a good save or a tough goal-against. He wanted to be a leader.

"He's always been a leader and our guys looked to him from the moment he arrived in camp," Johnston says. "He wanted to prove something. He led them all through the early going and now the guys look to him for the big plays."

It wasn't just for his leadership capabilities that the Penguins tabbed Lemieux; they recognised his talent and skill.

"His anticipation and play-reading abilities are just like Gretzky's," Johnston says. "He's a great passer and his attitude is terrific. He heard the knocks about his defencive skills and he knew it was a problem but he worked on it.

"Besides," jokes Johnston, "when you have the puck all the time you don't have to play defence."

Johnston is right in all his descriptions of Lemieux. At six foot four, Mario has an incredible reach that allows him to tease defenders with the puck, holding it just out of their reach. When his superb stick- and puck-handling skills are added, combined with his uncanny anticipation, the results can be startling, even for a Pittsburgh team that has often struggled to reach even mediocrity.

Though Pittsburgh failed to qualify for the playoffs in Mario's sophomore year, it wasn't for lack of his trying. Lemieux posted a 29-game scoring streak and scaled the 100-point mark for the second consecutive season.

Like Gretzky, Lemieux likes to set up behind the opposition's net. Islander Bill Smith is the goaltender.

DENIS SAVARD

Denis Savard's razzle-dazzle play leaves the opposition—and the fans—breathless.

For all his considerable talents, Lemieux is a quiet superstar. His on-ice wizardry is subtle, sometimes to the degree that only an experienced fan knows quite what he is seeing when Lemieux weaves his magic. Mario Lemieux will leave you stunned — "Did I just see that?" is the most usual response — but he won't pull you out of your seat.

For that, just watch **Denis Savard** of the Chicago Black Hawks. Called by many the most exciting player in the National Hockey League, Savard uses super-lative skating skills combined with terrific stick skills to amuse audiences and dis-combobulate opponents.

"Denis is one of those players who is not only a great hockey player but a player with charisma," explains Bob Pulford, Chicago's general manager and co-coach and the man who drafted Savard in 1980. "He's got that quality that keeps people coming out to see him play."

"There just isn't a better skater in the league than Denis Savard," says Lou Nanne, who, as general manager of the Norris Division rival Minnesota North Stars sometimes sees more of Savard than he cares to. "When Denis has the puck, he's got the ability to do a million things with it."

The idea that he is an entertainer in addition to being a top hockey player leaves Savard nonplussed, especially when he tries to explain just what it is that makes him so special.

"I'm still surprised when people say I'm exciting to watch, even after all this time," says Savard, a native of Verdun, Montreal. "Sometimes I'll try to put the puck between my legs or fake a pass, things like that. Or maybe I spin a few times. It seems to make people talk.

"But mostly it's just instinct," he continues. "I want to get the puck to a certain place, so I fake in and turn around on the defence because I feel the defence is confused. I don't do it to excite people. I know what I'm doing is different. I just don't know why."

Some hundred of miles to the east of Pittsburgh, the Detroit Red Wings boast a player similar to Mario Lemieux, not in style or execution, but in anticipation.

Management and fan anticipation, that is. For in the fall of 1983, though they wouldn't say so publicly, the Detroit Red Wings were pinning most, if not all, of their future success on 18-year-old **Steve Yzerman**.

They will tell you, the Detriot management will, that they were concerned with Yzerman's strength or lack thereof. When it became obvious to all that he had sufficient quantities of that, the management was worried that maybe Motown's new Little Stevie Wonder wouldn't be mature enough to contribute sufficiently to the Red Wings Renaissance.

Steve Yzerman, as if quoting from a television commercial, said, "BUNK!" All he did in his rookie year was set Red Wing rookie records for points and goals scored. Considering that the Red Wings once had a rookie by the name of Gordie Howe, that's not too shabby an accomplishment.

"Steve's maturity, presence and poise on the ice indicate just how good he'll be," says Nick Polano, now Detroit's assistant general manager but Yzerman's coach during the youngster's first two years in the NHL.

And what allows Yzerman to maintain that poise? "His puck-handling is his best asset because he has great hands," Polano answers. "He also has fantastic balance on his skates and has a great head for the game. He never has to be told anything

If there were any nonbelievers left after Yzerman's rookie season, they'd be hard to find. By the conclusion of the 1983–84 campaign, Yzerman had become the youngest player ever to play in the mid-season All-Star game, finished second to Buffalo's Tom Barrasso in voting for Rookie of the Year, and made Team Canada in the 1984 Canada Cup ahead of several established centres.

Yzerman was the fourth player picked overall in the 1983 entry draft. For their second pick, Detroit chose Lane Lambert, now Yzerman's roomate and one of his close friends.

"Steve is smooth as silk and that's what we call him, Silk. That's his nickname," says Lambert. "He's so good to begin with and he's just going to get better."

Says Polano, "He's got the ability to control a game, like a Denis Savard. That's the kind of player he's going to be for us for a long time."

PAT LAFONTAINE

Pat Lafontaine, the New York Islanders centre with the teen idol looks, is more than just a pretty face. Blessed with blinding speed, "The Roadrunner" averages almost a point per game.

ALAN HAWORTH

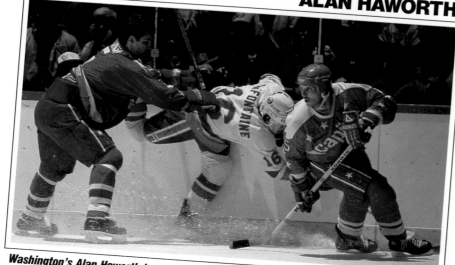

Washington's Alan Haworth had a career year in 1985–86, putting 34 goals past enemy netminders while collecting 39 assists. Here Washington's Rod Langway checks another centre of attention, the Islanders' Pat Lafontaine, to clear space for Haworth.

GIL PERRAULT

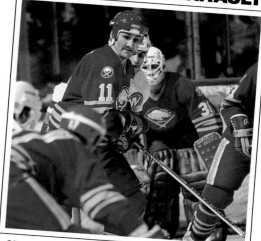

Gil Perrault, the original Buffalo Sabre, has scored 503 NHL goals and has 1,310 points. Though he turned 35 during the 1985–86 campaign, he remained the heart of the Sabres.

STEVE YZERMAN

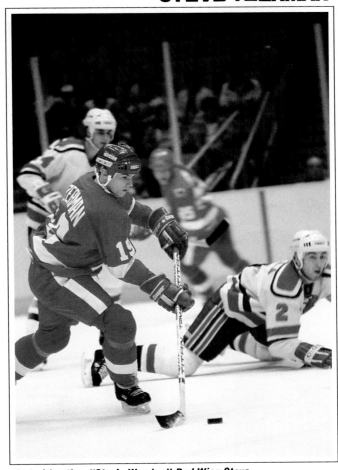

Detroit's other "Stevie Wonder," Red Wing Steve Yzerman often leaves his foes in the dust. Though injured in the second half of the 1985–86 season, Yzerman is still Detroit's main man in the pivot.

It is no accident that Yzerman's appearance keyed Detroit's playoff appearances in 1984 and 1985. After all, before his first season was a month old, he was centre for the Red Wings' number-one line, pivoting for John Ogrodnick on the left side and Ron Duguay at starboard.

And his play has developed too. Yzerman, always shifty, has become quicker and more confident on his skates. Unfortunately for Yzerman and Detroit, Little Stevie Wonder suffered a broken collarbone that made him miss the final 30 games of the 1985–86 season. But management remains confident about Yzerman's ability.

"He has an uncanny ability now to move out of the corners really quickly," Polano says. "He's tough to hit, so you see a lot of defencemen forced to pull him down."

The Detroit Red Wings aren't members of the NHL's elite yet, but if they are ever to knock on the Stanley Cup door, be sure that Steve Yzerman will have his hand on the knob.

In the same year the Red Wings drafted Yzerman, the New York Islanders selected a centre named **Pat LaFontaine**. To say that there is a contrast between the entrances of both Yzerman and LaFontaine into the NHL would be a gross understatement.

To begin with, Yzerman jumped right into the NHL while LaFontaine, a much-heralded scoring wizard, opted to play with the United States Olympic hockey team.

Where attention on Yzerman was quiet, LaFontaine was appearing in a national magazine, one of a number of subjects labeled "The Best of Everything."

Though the US faltered badly in its 1984 Olympic effort, LaFontaine returned to the New York Islanders for the final portion of the season.

In 15 regular season games, LaFontaine pumped in 13 goals for the then-defending Stanley Cup champions. Though the Islanders eventually succumbed to the Edmonton Oilers in the finals, surrendering their Stanley Cup for the first time, it was Pat LaFontaine who scored two goals in 22 seconds during the final game, serving notice that he would be an Islander force to contend with for seasons to come.

After all, LaFontaine notched 104 goals for the Verdun Canadiens of the Quebec League the year just prior to his drafting by the Islanders. And he scored 111 points in 58 pre-Olympic contests, earning the nickname Franny, short for Franchise. Why shouldn't he be a force?

Let us count the ways.

How about ligament damage to his left knee, suffered in a collision with Washington Capitals defenceman Scott Stevens during a Canada Cup exhibition game in August of 1984?

How about mononucleosis after recovering from the knee damage?

How about a disappointing 54 points in 67 games during his rookie year, a year that was supposed to see LaFontaine challenge Mario Lemieux for rookie pre-eminence?

"I got sick in training camp and I was never able to do the things I wanted to do," the handsome centre says. "When that mono hits you, it just knocks you out. They say it can stay in your system for six months or a year and I certainly felt like it did."

Not that any of the Islander personnel was discouraged by LaFontaine's relatively poor showing. Isles' general manager Bill Torrey (who, when he drafted LaFontaine said, "He's the kind of player who lifts you out of your seat. Pat's an exciting player, the type you're automatically attracted to") concurs.

"There's never been any doubts in our minds that Patty could perform here," Torrey says. "In fact, it's surprising that Patty was able to play as well as he did with the mono."

LaFontaine has always used his incredible skating speed to create his prolific scoring opportunities, but he has recently added a physical dimension that many observers felt was lacking in his game.

"I'm not getting knocked around as easily; maybe that's because the mono took some strength out of me," LaFontaine posits. "I've played like that before, I've just not had the opportunity to play like that in the NHL."

When presented with the opportunity in the 1985–86 season, only his sophomore NHL campaign, LaFontaine responded well. He scored goals and played a more consistently dangerous offensive game than during his freshman year, and finally began delivering on the promise he showed back in 1984.

By the end of the 1980–81 season, at the opposite end of the continent, the Winnipeg Jets had set several marks for National Hockey League futility, not the least of which was the record for most consecutive games without a win — 30.

Lose-a-peg, they came to be called. Clearly the situation called for some kind of improvement — a saviour, maybe. And in the draft of that year, Winnipeg's general manager, John Ferguson, found his hero. Since the Jets had the first pick overall, Fergie didn't have to look too far. "In my mind," recalls Fergie, "there was no doubt."

How could there be? The object of Ferguson's desire was a centre for the Cornwall Royals of the Ontario junior league who had scored 81 goals and led the Royals to the Memorial Cup, emblematic of junior hockey supremacy in Canada.

Into Winnipeg on his white horse rode **Dale Hawerchuk**, the man then called the best centre among mere mortals — Wayne Gretzky, of course, is simply superhuman.

In his first year for the Jets, Hawerchuk lived up to his billing, scoring 45 goals and adding 58 assists to become the youngest player ever to score 100 points in his rookie season.

"We were confident that Dale would be a great National Leaguer," Ferguson says. "He had all the offensive skills, plus great anticipation of the play and a great attitude."

The skills and anticipation earned him comparisons with Gretzky, with many experts feeling that one day Hawerchuk could contend with The Great One for the NHL's scoring title.

DALE HAWERCHUK

Winnipeg's Dale Hawerchuk, the first player chosen in the 1981 NHL entry draft. He led the Jets in scoring in 1985–86, notching 46 goals and 59 assists for 105 points.

BERNIE FEDERKO

Bernie Federko may not be a household name in your kitchen, but don't tell that to the St. Louis Blues. The Blues' leading scorer in 1985–86— Federko notched his third consecutive 100 + point season—is not often caught lying down on the job.

MARCEL DIONNE

The NHL's second all-time leading scorer, L.A.'s Marcel Dionne's talent is often overlooked by even the most knowledgeable hockey observers. Dionne is an offensive machine, scoring over 100 points in a season in eight of his 15 NHL years.

His attitude, on the other hand, had neutral observers comparing him with a whining baby. When, in his sophomore season (and with the Jets struggling) Hawerchuk felt he wasn't being given enough ice time by then coach Tom Watt, he whined, claiming that the lack of playing time cut down on his effectiveness.

When Hawerchuk's remarks were reported in the newspapers around the league, Watt, who had won the Jack Adams Trophy as Coach of the Year the previous season, left his Adams Trophy in Hawerchuk's stall as a message.

But general manager Ferguson agreed with Hawerchuk, and Watt was soon sent packing. Noticeable soon thereafter was a new Hawerchuk, a Hawerchuk who believed and played with new confidence and conviction.

Hawerchuk reached his young peak during the 1984–85 season. He finished third in the league in scoring (how about 53 goals and 77 assists for 130 points?), behind only Jari Kurri and — who else — Gretzky. The performance was so electrifying that the Professional Hockey Writer's Association voted Dale into second place for the league's Hart (MVP) Trophy.

One guess who the MVP award went to.

"To think of Dale as a loser because he didn't win this award and came in second to me is silly," Gretzky said as he accepted his sixth consecutive Hart Trophy. "He's a great player. Just look at what he's done for the Jets and where the team has gone since he's been there."

And though the Jets were swept out of the playoffs in 1985 by Gretzky's Edmonton Oilers, no one doubts how big a role Hawerchuk would have played.

"We were lucky not to have to play them with Dale Hawerchuk in the lineup. He makes all the difference for them," Gretzky admitted.

"There are other players who could score 200 points and I think they might do it soon," added The Great One to punctuate his compliment to Winnipeg's ace. "Mike Bossy could do it. And so could Dale Hawerchuk."

It is ironic that The Great One didn't mention one man who is as good a bet as Bossy and Hawerchuk to reach that hallowed 200-point mark. But, then again, Gretzky's oversight is typical.

After all, if **Marcel Dionne** wasn't overlooked, he wouldn't be looked at all.

It's unfortunate that Dionne, a man who entered the 1985–86 season as the NHL's third all-time scorer, and left it in second place, will probably see his name last longer not for his hockey exploits, but as the answer to many a trivia question. For example:

When Guy Lafleur was drafted first overall by the Montreal Canadiens in 1971, who was drafted second?

Who set an NHL points-by-rookies record and didn't win Rookie of the Year?

Who was the last man to win an NHL scoring crown before Wayne Gretzky — and on a technicality no less?

Yup, Dionne. Guilty on all counts.

Selected by the Detroit Red Wings in 1971, Dionne lost the Calder Trophy to Montreal's Ken Dryden. Dionne, who finally won the scoring championship after the 1979–80 season, actually had the same point total as Gretzky, but was awarded the Art Ross Trophy by virtue of having scored more goals.

In fact, throughout his entire magnificent carer, the NHL's most unknown super-star has been known for his goal-scoring, something many observers actually held against Dionne, citing an im-agined disdain for defence.

"I'd played and coached against Marcel and I had the same feelings about him that everybody else seems to have," says Dionne's coach on the Los Angeles Kings, Pat Quinn. "We thought he wasn't a team player, that he was more concerned with personal statistics than with the performance of the team.

"Well, not only is Marcel Dionne a great athlete and offensive player, he's a good defencive player and a team leader too."

It was Dionne who centred one of hockey's best lines during the late 1970s and early 1980s when he pivoted for left wing Charlie Simmer and right wing Dave Taylor to form the Triple Crown Line. The trio rolled up 161 goals and 352 points during the 1980–81 season and seemed destined to set records for scoring by a line when Simmer broke his leg in two places with just a month remaining on the schedule.

"Marcel is a great player and I don't know if he's gotten the recognition he deserves," says Simmer, now with the Boston Bruins. "He's unbe-lievably consistent, and he's done all his work for a lot of years on teams without a lot of talent.

"Marcel can do everything well," Simmer continues. "He can shoot, pass and skate, he can play physical and he has great quickness. He makes his moves at top speed."

Don't let anyone say that Marcel Dionne can't play defence, either. For many years, Dionne held the record for scoring the most short-handed goals in a season. You only get those one way and that's by playing defence against the other team's power-play unit.

There are other records in Dionne's sights now, marks that are certainly achievable. With his talent and durability (Dionne has yet to suffer a severe injury in over 15 years of NHL action, has never played fewer than 66 games in a season and has played at least eight full seasons), Marcel Dionne could very well top Phil Esposito for goals scored and move into second place in that cat-egory behind the legendary Gordie Howe.

And if he plays long enough, who knows? Maybe Marcel Dionne can catch Howe and earn, finally, the immortality he so richly deserves.

If Sutter is the ultimate for his all-around play, then Edmonton's **Mark Messier** must be a gift from heaven. Simply put, there is nothing Mark Messier cannot do.

Messier, originally a left wing but shifted to centre by Edmonton's general manager and coach Glen Sather, is an explosive skater, a superb goal-scorer and a relentless checker and hitter.

BRYAN TROTTIER

Called the NHL's best two-way centre, Bryan Trottier was an integral member of the New York Islander team that won four consecutive Stanley Cups at the decade's beginning.

Big, strong, fast and mean, the Oilers' Mark Messier can do just about everything on the ice. Originally a left wing, Messier was moved to centre by Oilers' coach Glen Sather.

"When I hit people," says the Oilers' Wayne Gretzky, "I just try to get in the way. But Mark, he *hurts* people." That's not surprising, considering Messier's six-foot, 205-pound build. Every inch of him is muscle; there's not a spare ounce anywhere, and Messier uses his strength to outstanding results.

Adds teammate Dave Lumley, "If Gretzky and Mark aren't one-two as the best in the world, I don't know who is."

Often lumped with Gretzky and Mike Bossy as the only three players that would run past compensation if the NHL had free agency, the best of Messier's years are ahead of him. In his NHL career, Messier — who has averaged better than a point a game throughout his tenure — has already been named an All-Star twice and captured the Conn Smythe Trophy as the playoff MVP during the Oilers' first run to the Stanley Cup.

It was during the 1984 Stanley Cup finals that Messier showed the world just how talented he is by almost singlehandedly dismantling the New York Islanders. Every clutch goal or tide-turning hit was delivered by Messier and his Smythe Trophy was well deserved.

"The Stanley Cup final is all it takes," says Messier of his motivation. "You don't get too many chances and they'd already beaten us. We knew we had to do it the next time."

"And it's great playing in my hometown. When I first got here [Messier played with Indianapolis and Cincinnati of the World Hockey Association before he was drafted by the Oilers in 1979] I didn't know how it was gonna turn out. But teammates my own age, plus friends and family around, make it nice to play here."

Nice enough for him to score 50 goals in 1981–82 and 48 more in 1982–83.

Messier, truly a hometown boy made good (he grew up in Edmonton), scored 26 points during the Oilers' Cup run. "I wanted to be like my dad," Mark says, referring to the elder Messier's professional — if minor league — career.

New York Ranger defenceman Reijo Ruotsalainen discovers that stopping Messier is no easy task.

"I was fortunate to have been on a young team that knew where it had been and where it wanted to go. We were patient and waited for everybody to come around and it's obviously paid off."

BARRY PEDERSON

Boston's Barry Pederson, who played only 22 games in the 1984–85 season because of an arm injury, rebounded strongly in 1985–86 with 29 goals and 47 assists. Pederson was the Bruins top-line centre.

Left Wings

Without aid on the port and starboard sides, those centres of attention wouldn't gain much attention at all. But left wings like Brian Sutter, Al Secord, John Ogrodnick and Michel Goulet are so good that they often make their centres look better, rather than the other way around.

As is the fashion among the Sutter brothers (there are five others sprinkled around the National Hockey League) **Brian Sutter** has become the heart and soul of the St. Louis Blues.

Brian is the eldest of the NHL's Sutter clan. His coach loves him.

"Sudsy is the epitome of our motto," says Jacques Demers. "Hard work and determination. I as a coach can preach it, but it's done on the ice. Sudsy has it." One look at Sutter on the ice is ample demonstration of that work ethic.

Sutter is just as liable to be slamming an opponent into the boards as he is to throw himself in front of a slapshot; just as likely to drop his gloves and fight as he is to create a fuss in front of the net to allow a teammate a clear path to the goal.

Drafted 20th overall by the Blues in 1976, Brian has more than modest goal-scoring ability, averaging a goal every two games over the length of his career. But as Demers says, Brian Sutter isn't a star just for his offensive achievements.

"I think he's the best captain in the league," Demers says, "because we outwork everybody else in the league and we do it with less talent. That's why I say Sutter is a great leader. He's the ultimate."

For Quebec's **Michel Goulet**, goal-scoring is paying off quite nicely, thank you. A refugee from the WHA, Goulet has blossomed into the best goal-scorer from the left side in the NHL.

"I guess I was always a goal-scorer," he says. "Even when I was a kid [Goulet was raised in Peribonk, Quebec — another hometown boy made good] I loved to score goals. I guess I was a bit of a showoff sometimes but scoring always came naturally to me."

. Tell us about it. In his final year of junior play, Goulet scored 73 goals before going on to an NHL career that has seen him hit four 50-goal seasons in the now-lost tradition of hockey's Flying Frenchmen.

Goulet has the grace on skates and the artistry that identified the Flying Frenchmen of the old Montreal Canadiens, even though Goulet toils for the Nordiques, Montreal's archrivals. Even to his peers, Goulet is something special.

BRIAN SUTTER

The eldest of the NHL's six Sutter brothers, Brian is the heart and soul of the St. Louis Blues. Blues coach Jacques Demers calls Sutter "the best captain in the league."

BRIAN PROPP

Their first choice in the 1979 NHL entry draft, Brian Propp has clearly paid dividends for the Philadelphia Flyers. Their leading scorer in 1985–86 (40 goals, 57 assists), Propp is always carefully watched by the opposition, in this case Kelly Hrudey and Denis Potvin of the New York Islanders.

CHARLIE SIMMER

Boston's Charlie Simmer has plenty of reasons to smile, and not only because he's married to a Playboy bunny. Simmer, despite missing 25 games in 1985–86 with various injuries, still potted 36 goals for the Bruins in his second season in Boston.

MICHEL GOULET

Quebec's Michel Goulet deserves all the attention he can get. Goulet has scored 221 goals over the last four seasons and may be the best-scoring left wing in the game.

"Michel has all the offensive skills associated with high-scoring French forwards," says Glen Sather, the Oilers' coach who was also the boss for Team Canada in the 1984 Canada Cup and who put Goulet on the port side of Wayne Gretzky and Rick Middleton.

"Plus, Goulet has the mobility and passing skills of a Swedish player and the strength and guts of an old-time NHL grinder. He's something."

"Sometimes I think Michel is a magician the way he gets into the open," says five-year linemate Dale Hunter. "Michel is the greatest and the strongest on the team. If I played every shift with him I would score a few more goals and certainly get a bushel of assists."

Adds coach Michel Bergeron, "Michel is a very versatile player, one who devotes much time and effort to checking, penalty-killing and being a good defensive forward. He is a great player on attack and also on defence."

"He convinced me to consider putting him on a line with the Stastnys," Bergeron continues. "He just did certain things better, his checking was superb and he got the puck in the corners better."

"Michel is our cleanup hitter. I put him on in the third period, whatever the situation, when defence or attack is needed. His strength and speed are unmatched and he's equally good at trying to score or trying to stop other guys from scoring. He may just be the best two-way forward in the NHL."

Selection to that Canada Cup team was an honour Goulet took to heart.

"The Canada Cup was my greatest experience so far," says Goulet. "I want to play on a Stanley Cup winner with the Nordiques, but even when we beat Montreal in the playoffs a few springs ago, I didn't feel as happy as I did the night we beat the Soviets."

And this final word from defenceman Larry Robinson, one of those Montreal Canadiens rivals. "Goulet is the MVP of the Nordiques. I respect Peter Stastny and the rest of their players, but Goulet does everything a player can do."

For the Detroit Red Wings, **John Ogrodnick** has proved as immensely valuable as Michel Goulet. The Red Wings' only certified offensive threat, Ogrodnick is on the threshold of greatness in the Motor City.

Teamed with pivot Steve Yzerman and converted centre Ron Duguay, Ogrodnick and mates have formed Detroit's best line — and one of the NHL's best, too.

Drafted by the Red Wings in 1979, Ogrodnick (at six feet and 190 pounds) uses good size and the ability to withstand powerful hits to score his goals. By his own admission, Ogrodnick is not a finesse player.

"I'm not a flashy player," he candidly admits. "I just get the puck and move it. I'm not the guy to stick-handle between two guys or around them and I'm not gonna try that because I can't do it."

Ogrodnick would be a perfect candidate for an American Express "Do you know me?" commercial because of his style and lack of flair. For Ogrodnick is one of the most underrated and overlooked players in the NHL.

That's surprising, for Ogrodnick is the Red Wings' record-holder for goals scored in a season, with 55 accumulated during the 1984–85 season — all from a willingness to take the punishment. As a reward, Ogrodnick was named to the NHL's first-team All-Star squad.

The 50-plus goal season was Ogrodnick's first, but he would have scaled those heights in the previous season had he not missed 16 games due to injury. Despite playing only 64 games in 1983–84, Ogrodnick finished with 42 goals, still the highest on the club.

"I don't mind not getting the exposure," Ogrodnick says. "That comes with success in the playoffs, from playing for winning teams. It really doesn't bother me."

"With a team like ours," says Red Wings general manager Jim Devellano, "which is a team not exactly known for scoring goals, John is very important. He gives us something we need. He's a solid player and good person. He has a lot of pride in what he accomplishes."

The last of our super left wings toils in Chicago, a blue-collar town. That's only fitting because **Al Secord** is a blue-collar player.

Drafted originally by the Boston Bruins in 1978, when Secord got to the NHL and Beantown early that season, the thing he did best was accumulate penalty minutes. In two seasons with the Bruins, Secord totalled almost 300 minutes in penalties; his two-season goal tab was a whopping 39.

JOHN OGRODNICK

One of the consistent—and few—bright spots on a usually dreary Detroit Red Wings team, John Ogrodnick is on the threshold of NHL stardom. He has already posted one 50-goal season, to go along with two 40-goal and two 30-goal years.

ANTON STASTNY

Less flamboyant than brother Peter, but just as important to the success of the Nordiques, is Anton Stastny. The Czech expatriate has totaled 191 goals in five NHL seasons.

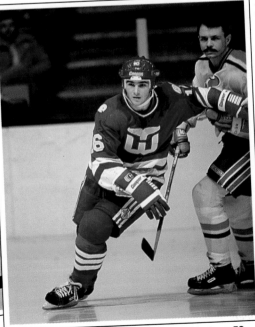

SYLVAIN TURGEON

Hartford's Sylvain Turgeon is destined to be a 50-goal scorer for the Whalers. Fast, strong and armed with a deadly shot, Turgeon rang up 45 goals in the 1985–86 campaign, just his third NHL season.

AL SECORD

Hawks' "Macho Man" Al Secord finds time to relax in the penalty box, a place where he's quite at home. Secord's temper sometimes gets the best of him, to the tune of 1,436 career penalty minutes.

EDDY BEERS

Eddy Beers, signed as free agent by the Calgary Flames, now gives a strong physical presence to his current club, the St. Louis Blues. Beers has a scoring touch too, posting seasons of 36 and 28 goals.

But credit a trade to Chicago (in exchange for then Bruin defenseman Mike O'Connell) with triggering Secord's goal-scoring talent. Though he still attracted penalty minutes like a magnet attracts iron, Secord struck for 44 goals in his first full season with the Hawks and 54 goals in 1982–83.

His penalty-minute total for those first two seasons in Chicago, by the way, was a huge 483. So despite his perfect game attendance in those two years, Secord actually spent over eight games in the penalty box. Tells you a little something about Secord's style.

A quiet and gentlemanly fellow off the ice, Secord throws his six foot one inch, 205-pound body at anything and everything on the ice; most of what he throws are his fists.

"An aggressive style of play is what got me here," says Secord. "If I play aggressively and physically, then goals will come for me. If I'm banging, the goals will take care of themselves. If I start worrying about goal-scoring, that'll take away from my physical game and then I'll be worthless."

Originally a defenceman in junior play, Secord moved to the wing and the results have been apparent. With the exception of two seasons when he suffered from pulled abdominal muscles (1983–84 and 1984–85), Secord has always played a hard-nosed game; as predicted, the goals have taken care of themselves. He rebounded in 1985–86, scoring 30-plus goals.

Part of that equation has been Secord's ability to motivate himself more readily since he's been in the Windy City, something he didn't always do in Boston.

"I didn't maintain my intensity in Boston," Secord admits. "You know, I'd play a good two or three games, score a couple of goals, and then I'd let up and coast. I'd slack off and it would take me three or four more games to get back into a groove.

"After I got sent to the minors and then when I came to Chicago, I knew I had to prepare mentally for each game. I didn't want to waste another opportunity. I concentrate on what my job is so I don't have to think on the ice — everything comes naturally."

"Al is a very underrated hockey player," says line-mate Denis Savard. "He can skate and shoot and we contribute to each other's success. The other guys around the league have respect for him too, because he works so hard."

Secord knows that hard work and dedication are what has made him successful in America's Second City, and because of that work ethic, Chicago truly is Al Secord's kind of town.

And for Sutter, Secord, Goulet, and Ogrodnick to be named as the NHL's best left wingers? That's more than just a left-handed compliment.

Right Wings

Throughout the history of the National Hockey League, certain truths have been held to be self-evident. One of those truths is that many of the game's most exciting and historic figures played the right wing.

If there's any doubt about that (and yes, many exciting players have played other positions) just take a partial look at the right wing list. Three names will convince even the staunchest doubters:

Gordie Howe. Maurice Richard. Guy Lafleur.

See, we told you.

Nowadays, there is no dearth of quality right wing talent, much of it falling into the Super Scorer class. But even without those super-scorers, men like Dave Taylor, Dino Ciccarelli, Paul MacLean and Steve Larmer are carving a niche for themselves beside some of hockey's all-time greats.

The story of **Dave Taylor**, for example, has been repeated so many times it's almost gained the quality of a fairy tale. And in some ways Taylor's entrance to the NHL is a make-believe one.

While a sophomore at Clarkson College, Taylor was drafted by the Los Angeles Kings in the 14th round of the 1975 amateur draft, number 210 overall.

You don't play pro hockey from that draft position, you apply for a mortician's license. Yet Taylor pushed, and after just seven games in the minors he found himself laboring for the L.A. Kings. After a short stint on another line, followed by a longer one in the stands, Taylor was put on Marcel Dionne's right side, a place he's been ever since.

"It was the type of thing we all joked about in college," Taylor remembers with a laugh. "Because I was drafted as a sophomore, guys would say, 'Well, next year when you're up there with Marcel. . .'

"That was the joke. But the joke was on them because that's how it worked out."

Did it ever. After the duo played with a number of left wingers, Charlie Simmer — now of the Boston Bruins — happened along and the trio suddenly became the Triple Crown Line, one of the most successful and exciting trios ever to lace on skates.

"As I came up through hockey," says Taylor, explaining how he got to and stayed in the pros, "in both minor hockey and college, I saw a lot of players that I thought were better than me. But I'm in the NHL and they're not.

"You've got to work harder as each grade comes, you've got to keep improving. That's how you become a great player."

Working hard is indeed how Dave Taylor has made his mark on the NHL. Of course, his habit of scoring goals (he has broached the 40-goal mark at least three times in his NHL career) and playing tough hockey (his penalty-minute total still exceeds his point total) hasn't hurt either.

"I try to play hard-nosed," Taylor says. "It's how we practiced. We wanted to be able to do everything well, so if you had the chance to score, you scored. If you had the chance to hit, you hit. I think that's the key to being a good player."

Steve Larmer of the Black Hawks joins Taylor in the all-work, no-play category of performer.

"I just kept working, working, working," says Larmer, a Peterborough, Ontario, native, commenting on his attitude when he was promoted to the NHL from the American Hockey League, after twice playing with the Hawks for stretches of four and then three games.

"I never knew what would happen to me and I didn't really feel comfortable until after Christmas [of his rookie NHL year]," Larmer continues. "I wouldn't be where I am today without the year in the American League. I don't think I could have gone right from junior to Chicago because I had too much to learn.

DAVE TAYLOR

L.A.'s Dave Taylor used to dream about playing alongside super-centre Marcel Dionne. Taylor made the most of his chance when he got it and he eyes future success.

STEVE LARMER

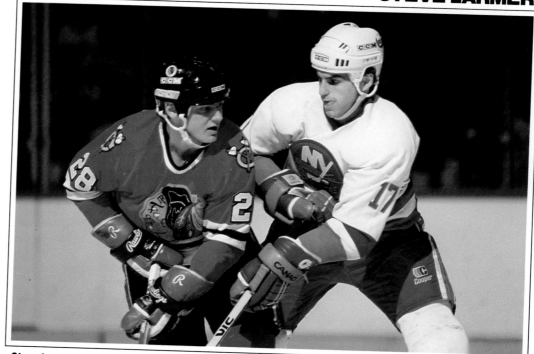

Steve Larmer, here going one-on-one with the Islanders' Greg Gilbert, teams with centre Denis Savard and left wing Al Secord to wreak havoc on the opposition.

Calgary's Lanny McDonald has one of the NHL's best slapshots. McDonald burned the Flames' opposition for 28 goals during the 1985–86 season, and has scored as many as 66 goals in a year. He also has the NHL's best mustache.

LANNY MCDONALD

DINO CICCARELLI

Dino Ciccarelli was a shooting North Star in 1985–86, scoring 44 goals in a big rebound from his previous year's effort. Regarded by many as spoiled, Ciccarelli quieted his critics with a return to the form that notched 55 goals in 1981–82.

"The big things were learning to play in our end of the rink and adjusting to playing in a tougher league against a lot of older guys. Mentally, I also grew in that year. I learned a lot about myself."

The American Hockey League must have taught Larmer well, for in his first NHL season Steve bagged 43 goals and 47 assists for 90 points and the Calder Trophy as the NHL's best rookie. "I was just hoping for a spot on the club," Larmer says innocently.

"Steve did have to get used to the speed at first," says linemate Al Secord. "And it's difficult playing with Denis [Savard, the line's centre] in the beginning because he's so dazzling. But Steve is the type of guy who just keeps working until he gets something right."

If Larmer got something right in his rookie year, his 1984–85 season requires some redefining of the term. After slumping to 35 goals in his sophomore year, Larmer came back exceptionally strong as a junior, potting 46 goals to lead the team in that category.

Certainly, Larmer isn't doing anything wrong at right wing for Chicago.

Labouring for Chicago's Norris Division rivals, the Minnesota North Stars, is one of the game's most colourful, talented and enigmatic players.

Dino Ciccarelli made his mark long before he made the NHL, scoring 72 goals and 142 points in juniors during the 1977–78 season. Three seasons later, Dino was a hero as the North Stars marched to the Stanley Cup finals.

Ciccarelli scored 14 goals and added seven assists in 19 playoff games that year, setting a number of rookie scoring records even though the Stars fell to the Islanders in five games during that final series.

The next year's campaign — 1981–82 — was a remarkable one for the young man from Ontario, then just 20 years old. He poured in 55 goals and added 51 assists for 106 points.

"How'd I do it?" echoes Ciccarelli. "Well, for one thing, you won't see me deke through a whole team. I'm just best around the net, anticipating when and how the puck will come, how to move to the right spot at the right time."

Though he hasn't hit in the 50-goal range since, Ciccarelli has scored in the top 30s several times, and rebounded in 1985–86 with 40-plus goals, while developing another part of his game.

"I have a bad reputation defencively," he acknowledges candidly, "though I know I've improved my defencive play. But the rep is there. I've concentrated a lot more on every shift because if we concentrate on cutting down the other team's chances, then the puck will turn over and we'll get chances.

"I don't like to set a certain target for goals, I just like to get my opportunities. I just like to do what I can do to get opportunities. If I create the opportunities, I'm happy."

Ciccarelli suffered a broken leg in junior, an injury severe enough to require surgery and intensive rehabilitation before Dino was ready to play hockey again.

After demonstrating his ability in junior at the age of 19 and after rehab, North Stars general manager Lou Nanne signed Ciccarelli as a free agent (the winger had been overlooked in the entry draft because of his injury).

"Best move I ever made as general manager," says Nanne. "He's important to us in a dual capacity. Number one as a productive scorer and secondly as a personality. If you like the North Stars you'll like him."

The crowd at the Met Center in Bloomington took Dino to its heart during that Stanley Cup playoff rush, screaming "Di-no, Di-no," every time he touched the puck and waving around Dino the Dinosaur dolls, the symbol of a defunct oil company.

But Ciccarelli is anything but defunct, and once again he's heating up North Star fans around the league with his exciting, emotional play.

JOE MULLEN

Twice a 40-goal scorer for the St. Louis Blues, Joe Mullen was sent packing to the Calgary Flames in a multi-player deal in mid-season. If the New York native was affected by the trade his performance didn't betray it, as he collected 44 goals and his third consecutive 40-goal season.

JOHN ANDERSON

The epitome of "have bag, will travel" in 1984–85, John Anderson was traded twice within a season's span. Sent to Quebec by Toronto during the off-season, Anderson was dispatched to Hartford shortly before the season's end. His arrival in Hartford keyed the Whalers playoff efforts, as Hartford sent Quebec to an early vacation courtesy of a 3–0 sweep in the opening round of the playoffs.

RICK MIDDLETON

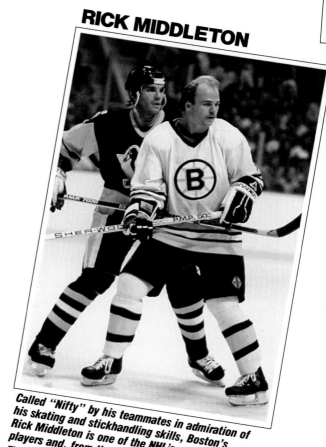

Called "Nifty" by his teammates in admiration of his skating and stickhandling skills, Rick Middleton is one of the NHL's smoothest players and, from the blueline in, one of the most dangerous.

PAUL MACLEAN

Winnipeg's Paul Maclean teams with Dale Hawerchuk and Brian Mullen to form one of the NHL's most effective trios. Though hampered by pulled stomach muscles in the 1985–86 season, Maclean still played 69 games and tallied 56 points.

There are a number of noticeable things about Winnipeg's superb starboard gunner **Paul MacLean**. But for novelty, the most interesting detail is that he was born in that hotbed of hockey talent, Grostenquin, France.

Aside from that, MacLean is your average, everyday 40-goal scorer, despite the fact that his original team, the St. Louis Blues, sent him home from training camp in 1978.

MacLean went back to college in Canada, then tried out for and made the 1980 Canadian Olympic team, an experience he credits with getting him to the NHL.

"The two years with the Olympic team put me in the NHL because my skills weren't good enough for me to get here on my own," says MacLean. "Good coaching and international competition — there's nothing to compare to it. And the intensity of the Olympics, because it's so short, taught me to go out and work every shift."

At six feet and 190 pounds, MacLean, who plays on a line with super centre Dale Hawerchuk, is a digger. His strength serves him exceptionally well in front of the net and he uses both size and strength in the opposing goal mouth on Jets power plays.

"I just try to get the puck to Dale and let him play with it for a while," says MacLean. "I do the bulk of my work in the corners and around the net." The bulk of Mac's work turns into Jets goals. Take 1984–85 as an example.

Paul scored 41 goals and added 60 assists that season, a year when the Jets challenged, but succumbed to, the Edmonton Oilers in the Smythe Division finals of the Stanley Cup playoffs. That point total means Big Mac was involved in 101 goals for Winnipeg, an eye-opening amount.

Paul rounded out the top dozen NHL scorers that year and he's the only Jet — aside from Dale Hawerchuk — to broach the 100-point mark.

But 1984–85 was far from Paul's only productive year. Just the year before, MacLean had cracked the 40-goal barrier for the first time, turning on the light 40 times and assisting on 31 other goals. Even during 1985–86, when he suffered pulled abdominal muscles and his team faltered badly in the standings, MacLean performed well. So consistency as well as toughness and scoring ability are within MacLean's makeup.

So there they are, four of the game's best on the starboard side. And Paul MacLean, Dino Ciccarelli, Dave Taylor and Steve Larmer are doing their best to become stars in the NHL's all-time right wing pantheon.

BENGT GUSTAFSSON

"Magic" to his teammates, Washington's Bengt Gustafsson has a habit of making the puck disappear—behind the enemy goaltender. Gustafsson's now-you-see-it-now-you-don't puckhandling ability led him to 75 points in 70 games during the 1985–86 season, until a check from the Islanders' Denis Potvin put him on the shelf with a broken leg. He is playing in Sweden during the 1986–87 season.

Defencemen

Once upon a time, in a land called the National Hockey League, there lived a big, scary creature. He wasn't very fast and many people thought he wasn't very smart. But he was very big and strong.

He was called a *defenceman*. All he did was hit people and protect his goaltender and block shots and, sometimes, play a little rough. And when the defencemen were playing, games would end with scores like 2−1 or 3−2. Sometimes even as high as 5−2.

But as time went by, and a new creature named Bobby Orr arrived on the hockey scene, defencemen began to die out. The big, scary defencemen proved too slow to catch the new creatures, creatures that could skate better and move the puck better and score better.

Of course, the Orr creatures didn't all play defence as well as the big scary defencemen did, but no one seemed to care, especially since the fans enjoyed what they were watching, which was a lot more scoring. And now games ended with scores like 7−4, or 6−5 or 10−3.

Yet a strange thing started to happen, despite those high-scoring games — or probably because of them. Defencemen began to reappear. Yes, slowly though it occurred, defencemen began to dot the horizon again.

Players like Larry Robinson, Brad Marsh, Rod Langway and Ken Morrow returned to the scene and brought with them the lost arts of body checking and shot-blocking and goalie protecting.

DEFENCIVE DEFENCEMEN

The best of these returning titans, when he was at his best, was **Larry Robinson**. At six foot three and 220 pounds, Robinson was the ultimate guardian of the defencive zone. He won the Norris Trophy, emblematic of the league's best defence-man, twice, was named to the post-season All-Star team five times, and won the Conn Smythe Trophy as the playoff MVP in 1978.

With Robinson in the back-field, the Montreal Canadiens captured four consecutive Stanley Cups from 1976 through 1979 and, when Les Habitants began their swing back into the NHL's elite class after several years in the dumps, their revitalization was coincidental with Robinson's own.

LARRY ROBINSON

Eagle-eyed Larry Robinson has regained the form that makes him one of the NHL's premier defencemen. Montreal's Big Bird once again became the backbone of the Canadiens, patrolling the defensive zone with authority, as well as expanding the offensive element of his game. Here, he wrestles with New Jersey's Jan Ludvig.

"My main concern has always been to be a defencive hockey player," says Robinson, who has actually put some good numbers on the board as a defencive defenceman, scoring 19 goals and 85 points in 1977, and has also had several 60-plus point seasons.

"I think too much emphasis is placed on the number of points a defenceman scores," Robinson admits. "A lot of defencemen have different situations on their own teams. Denis Potvin is on the power play all the time, for example.

BARRY BECK

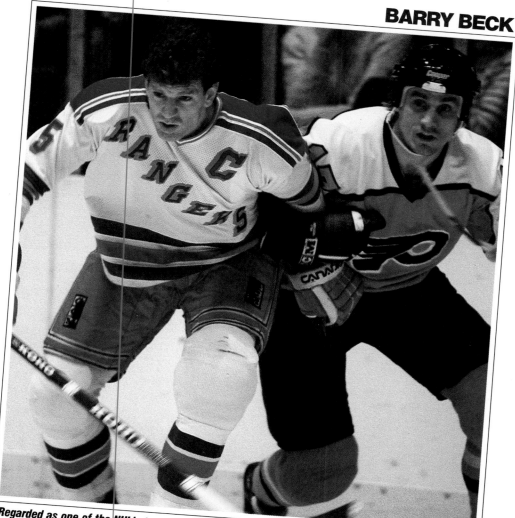

Regarded as one of the NHL's toughest defence-men, New York Ranger Barry Beck struggled to return from injury in 1985. When healthy, Beck is tremendously strong and is especially effective in front of his own net.

"A guy like Serge Savard [now Robinson's boss in Montreal but a former teammate] was never on the power play and he was an outstanding defenceman."

If a turning point in Robinson's recent past must be found, a clue as to his reemergence as an NHL force (and Robinson was back to his old self in the 1985–86 campaign, posting All-Star figures), look to the Stanley Cup playoff series between Robinson's Canadiens and the rival Quebec Nordiques in the 1984 playoffs.

With one of Quebec's Stastny brothers carrying the puck out of the Nordiques zone, Robinson came cross-ice and belted the Nordique clear into next week, to say nothing of six feet in the air, 10 feet backward and out of the game.

In a tough intra-divisional series such as that (Montreal eventually won after six games) with all its incumbent pressure, Robinson found himself playing some of the best hockey of his career.

"Larry's brought a winning attitude to the rest of our team," says mate Guy Carbonneau. "More than giving us confidence, he still does a great job for us. He still has the ability to turn a game around. He'll carry the puck when we're in trouble and settle things down to take the pressure off some of the younger guys."

"My role here has never really changed," Robinson says. "The only difference between now and the days when Serge was here is that then I might carry the puck a little more or lead a few rushes. Now I let the kids carry the puck more and I concentrate on other aspects of the game."

One of those kids who sort of outgrew the master played with Robinson for four years in Montreal before being traded to another franchise. The student is coming into his own now.

Rod Langway, currently the NHL's prototypical defenceman, learned his craft by watching Robinson in the seasons they played together in Montreal, 1979–1982.

In the fall of 1982, in what has developed into one of the blockbuster deals in the history of the NHL (to say nothing about being one of the greatest steals ever perpetrated by one general manager against another), Washington Capital general manager David Poile, on the job for just 10 days, swapped forward Ryan Walter and defenceman Rick Green to Montreal in exchange for Langway and fellow defence-man Brian Engblom, along with forwards Doug Jarvis and Craig Laughlin.

All Langway did was mature into the best defence-man in the NHL, as evidenced by his two-year hold on the Norris Trophy.

"The big thing that came out of that was really an intangible," Poile says. "Rod became our leader on the ice and off the ice. When he got here, he recognised the chance he had to put Rod Langway on the map. When we got the players from Montreal, we knew they had a winning attitude."

Langway started his hockey career at the age of 12, almost over the hill for anyone who intends to play hockey professionally. He did it only because everyone else in his Randolph, Massachu-setts hometown was playing too.

ROD LANGWAY

Rod Langway, the Capital's captain, is also Washington's Secretary of Defence. Simply, he is without flaw defencively. Before Langway's arrival in Washington (from Montreal, via trade) the Capitals had never made the playoffs; they have been to the NHL's post-season party ever since.

MIKE RAMSEY

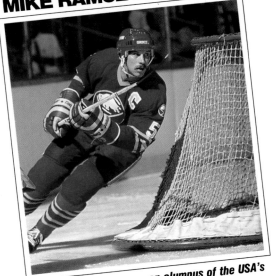

Buffalo's Mike Ramsey, an alumnus of the USA's 1980 gold-medal Olympic team, has added sta-bility to the Sabres defencive corps. He was Buffalo's first choice in the 1979 NHL entry draft.

In high school Langway was a catcher and pitcher for his baseball team and in college he became a tremendous linebacker, so good that the National Football League scouts were telling Rod's friends to tell him to forget about hockey. "Play football and get rich," they said.

But during that time, while Langway was at the University of New Hampshire — playing both football and hockey — he was drafted by the World Hockey Association Birmingham Bulls and by the NHL's Canadiens.

Fatefully, the Bulls offered Rod more money and he signed with the WHA club. Fatefully, because Langway admits he did most of his learning in Birmingham.

"I learned more about hockey that one year I played in Birmingham than I did in any other season I played," Langway says, his voice still touched by the telltale New England accent.

By the next season, Langway had agreed to play for Montreal and, after spending just 18 games on their Nova Scotia farm club, Rob joined the Habs for their last successful defence of the Stanley Cup in the spring of 1979.

Says Pierre Larouche, a former teammate of Langway's in Montreal: "He's just so incredibly dedicated. He leads by example and he has the heart of a lion." Adds Edmonton's Wayne Gretzky, "Rod knows how to prepare mentally for whoever he's playing. So, when the guy is coming at him, he knows how to play and he's never out of position."

Langway himself knows how beneficial his trade to Washington was. Forget about how he practically carried the Capitals into their first-ever playoff series the spring of his first Washington year. He knows too, that without this trade he would never have been given an opportunity to show how good he could be.

As he said on the June 1983 night when he accepted his first Norris Trophy at the NHL's annual awards dinner, "I'd like to thank David Poile for making the trade, and I'd like to thank Irving Grundman [then Montreal's managing director] for accepting it."

KEVIN LOWE

The defence of the Edmonton Oilers is often overshadowed by their goal-scoring exploits. But Kevin Lowe is one of the NHL's best, adding substance to the NHL's Team Style.

Like Langway, the New York Islanders' **Ken Morrow** has always been a winner. In fact, for the five years between 1979 and 1983, Morrow forgot how to lose.

Tall (six foot four) and with one of the longest reaches in the NHL, Morrow was drafted by the Islanders in the fourth round of the 1976 amateur draft while still playing for the Falcons of Bowling Green University. It was as a Falcon that Morrow suffered that loss in 1979, losing to Minnesota in the NCAA regional play-offs.

"After that, it was like I won everything and I'd forgotten how to lose," says Morrow who sports a heavy beard and is called Wolfman by his teammates. "At the Olympic trials, my team [Great Lakes] won. At the pre-Olympic B team tournament, we won that. In the Olympics we won the gold medal. And then in May of 1980, we won the Stanley Cup. I'd been in four tournaments in a year and I won all four."

Though he played only 18 regular season games with the Islanders when he joined them following the USA's successful gold medal conquest at Lake Placid, Morrow was as integral a member of the team as Mike Bossy or Bill Smith.

"Ken is the kind of player every winning team must have," says Herb Brooks, Morrow's coach on that gold-medal—winning squad. "He was very mature when he joined us and he was also very reliable. I always knew where to find him when I looked and what he would do and not do. Just real dependable."

So impressive was Morrow that Islander general manager Bill Torrey was able to deal away veteran defence-man Dave Lewis, along with forward Billy Harris, for centre Butch Goring, the man who would become the Islanders sparkplug during their run to four straight Stanley Cups.

Like Ramsey an alumnus of Team USA, Ken Morrow joined the Islanders immediately follow-ing the 1980 Olympics and went right on the Stanley Cup parade. With a long reach, Morrow is extremely tough to beat; he is one of the NHL's best shot-blockers.

KEN MORROW

Morrow stepped right into the lineup and has been there since, despite knee injuries that have severely hampered his already limited mobility. But despite his lack of skating speed or skill, Morrow has developed into one of the NHL's best defencive defencemen because of his reach, his shot-blocking talents and his ability to be in the right place at the right time to thwart an offensive flurry.

"When you stick-check the puck away from someone, you need good timing and Morrow has that," says Edmonton's Glenn Anderson. "He's strong on his skates and very difficult to get around and he has that long reach. Just when you start getting into position to do something, Ken pokes the puck off your stick. He did that to us a lot the first time we played in the finals."

By the time the Islanders and the Oilers met in the 1983 Stanley Cup final series, Anderson and his buddies knew that the New Yorkers would be a thorn in their collective Albertan sides, for it was Morrow's overtime goal that eliminated the Oilers in six games during the 1981 playoff campaign, the year the Islanders won their second Stanley Cup.

When the Islanders and the Oilers met in 1983, the Oilers had blossomed into the NHL's club of the future while the Islanders were one step from being tossed on the trash heap.

But the Islanders weren't buying any of that over-the-hill stuff. In swift fashion they swept the Oilers out of the finals in four straight games to annexe New York's fourth consecutive Stanley Cup.

By the way, in that series a defenceman named Morrow outscored a forward named Gretzky three goals to zero. "We had a lot of critics and I think we silenced them," Morrow would say after that Cup win. "I think we showed how special a team we are."

And Ken Morrow has shown how special he is, too.

LEE FOGOLIN

Lee Fogolin, originally a Buffalo Sabre, joins teammate Kevin Lowe in a triumph of substance over style. Fogolin too is vastly under-rated; and his steadiness and experience have had a calming effect on the young Oilers.

BRAD MARSH

Some 90 miles down the New Jersey Turnpike, about two hours from the Nassau Coliseum, lies the Philadelphia Spectrum. Inside, dressed in Flyer orange and black, lumbers defensive dinosaur **Brad Marsh**.

Actually, lumbers is an unfair word, for Marsh — acquired by the Flyers from the Flames for Mel Bridgman during the 1981 season — has benefitted from power-skating lessons and superior coaching. Still, no one would confuse Marsh with Bobby Orr.

"I think if you put Brad Marsh in the role of a defencive defenceman, you do a little injustice to his game," says New York Rangers head coach Ted Sator. Sator should know; he's the one who improved Marsh's skating while with the Flyers as an assistant coach.

"Brad rushes the puck pretty darn well and he has a good shot. But defencively, shot-blocking is one thing Brad does exceptionally well. That's a lost art."

Though Sator wouldn't admit to it, other NHLers will tell you that Marsh is also the league's best holder. But that's to be expected from a guy who should be part of the goaltenders' union for all the stops he makes.

Careening helmetless around the ice, Marsh will bang an opponent here, grab a stick there, toss a cross-check and block a shot, all before getting more than 10 feet from his bench.

"He does have that innate leadership ability," Sator notes. "You don't always see that just with his performance on the ice. Sometimes it's what he doesn't do — like he doesn't put himself in awkward positions even when he's rushing the puck."

Philadelphia's Brad Marsh, doing what he does best: holding. Marsh will sacrifice his body to prevent opposing forwards from getting a clear shot at the Flyers' goaltenders, stopping so many shots that his teammates call him another goalie.

REED LARSON

He may have changed uniforms (Larson is now a Boston Bruin), but the style remains the same. Larson is most effective at the point in the offensive zone, terrorizing goaltenders with a shot so hard someone once said, "It could rip the legs off an elephant."

Brad is seldom caught out of position, though truth be told, that's probably because he hardly tries. Perhaps more than anyone else, Marsh is a dinosaur, a throwback to the days when a defenceman's job was to prevent scoring. To do that, Marsh will fling himself in front of pucks screaming toward him at speeds of 100 mph and deflect them with his chest, arms or legs. And yes, his head too.

"I don't think about getting hurt," Marsh says, "because if I did I couldn't play that way and that's my game. I know what my limitations and capabilities are and I try to play the game I can play."

Says Bob McCammon, now Edmonton's assistant coach but then the man who traded for Marsh in 1981, "We not only got a good defenceman, we acquired a leader."

They are large and unwieldy, these dinosaurs, and perhaps they are growing old too. But without them for contrast, we'd never be able to appreciate Bobby Orr's clones — the defencemen of the new generation.

New Generation Defencemen

They have names like Denis Potvin, Mark Howe, Reijo Ruotsalainen, Doug Wilson, Phil Housley, Paul Coffey and Ray Bourque. Some play for champions, others for also-rans. But they all have one thing in common: Bobby Orr.

Without Orr, the legend who almost singlehandedly created the style of hockey played today, none of these seven fine defencemen would be as outstanding as they are.

For it was Orr who changed the game, allowing defencemen to become not only part of the attack, but in some cases the attack itself. It was Orr who won eight consecutive Norris trophies as the National Hockey League's finest defenceman, a legacy continued by the Islanders' Denis Potvin, the Hawks' Doug Wilson and the Oilers' Paul Coffey.

There have been many players who have graduated from the junior and minor leagues with big-league reputations, and there have been many players who never fulfilled those big-league expectations.

One who has succeeded in living up to his billing is **Denis Potvin**. From the time he scored his first Islander goal as a rookie in 1973 (and later went on to win the NHL's Rookie of the Year award) to the point in 1985 when he broke Orr's scoring record for career points and goals by a defenceman, Potvin has always been a notch above all but a handful of his NHL compatriots.

Potvin was the Islander's first choice in the 1973 draft and the first choice overall, a dubious privilege gained by the Islanders based on their sorrowful performance during the 1972–73 season, their first in the NHL.

He was not always a favourite of his compatriots. He alienated his suburban teammates by demonstrating a passion for the city life of art galleries, museums, operas and fine restaurants. He alienated the world when he proclaimed that, in an international series, he, not Orr, deserved to have been voted MVP.

Now in his 30s, with Norris trophies and four Stanley Cups behind him and a Hall of Fame berth ahead, Potvin has mellowed. He has gained control of a high blood pressure disorder that threatened to abbreviate his career. He is on good footing with his mates, having gained their confidence and support during the 1979–80 season; it is no coincidence that the Islanders captured their first Stanley Cup in the first year Denis Potvin felt himself a full team member. Now Potvin feels like he's arrived.

"When I turned 30, it was the best birthday I ever had," he says. "My 20s were tough for me, with a lot of growing pains. I'm happy to be in my 30s now and I wouldn't trade that for anything."

It was in the golden year of his 32nd birthday that Potvin etched himself into hockey immortality, wresting from Orr two records the former Bruin great had once posted.

"Individual achievements and records are great things to have," Potvin says, "but just to be in the company of a Bobby Orr is a great compliment to me."

DENIS POTVIN

No defenceman, with the arguable exception of Edmonton's Paul Coffey, is better with the puck than the Islanders' Denis Potvin. In the twilight of a Hall of Fame career, that look up-ice still means trouble for an opposing goaltender.

PAUL COFFEY

For a time during the Orr era, each new offensive prodigy was billed as "the next Orr." Yet Potvin's accomplishments aside (difficult as it is), there is another star who may well eclipse the records of Orr and Potvin together. In fact, if there hadn't been an Orr, Edmonton's **Paul Coffey** who in 1985–86, set a new record for goals scored in a season by a defenceman, would most certainly have become the standard for offensively oriented rearguards.

"When Paul gets the puck he takes off for the other end and plays like *two* guys," says Lou Nanne, general manager of the Minnesota North Stars. "A two-on-one led by Coffey is really a three-on-one, because that's how good Paul is. He certainly is the fastest skater the NHL has ever had. In a way, Paul might be better than Bobby, because Bobby only played a couple of seasons with good knees and we never did get to see what he might have become. As an attack defenceman, Paul is the best of all time."

The opposite of damning with faint praise are such extravagant compliments, but Coffey might just be worth it. After all, Coffey hit for 126 points in the 1983–84 season, just 13 points behind Bobby Orr's record for points scored in a season by a defenceman.

"What I think puts Paul in his own class are his one-on-one rushes," says Edmonton general manager Glen Sather, who played with Orr in Boston during the later 1960s. "Paul goes right to the opposition net, but he does it smartly and without selfishness. Orr had great acceleration, but not as quick as Coffey's."

Coffey's reaction to the comparisons, unlike that of a young Potvin, is humility.

"I'm flattered, but I still think I have things to learn about playing defence," says the 25-year-old Ontario native. "I've said it before, when he came into the NHL he revolutionized hockey. A guy like Orr comes along only once."

If not for Bobby Orr, Edmonton's Paul Coffey would be the standard by which offensively skilled defencemen would be judged. Though in the spotlight for his scoring wizardry, Coffey is more than adequate in his own zone too.

The only thing missing for Coffey was the recognition of the media, those folks who present the NHL's trophies at the end of the season. For two years a debate raged between the Paul Coffey–Rod Langway camps as to who was the better defenceman and thus more deserving of the Norris Trophy.

After two years of Langway's rule, Coffey annexed the silverware in 1985, following a superb season that began with a Team Canada, Canada Cup victory and ended with the Oilers' second straight Stanley Cup.

To Coffey, winning the Norris Trophy was vindication for a career often criticised as too strong offensively and too weak defensively and therefore incomplete and inadequate.

"I think I convinced the writers and the fans when we won the Canada Cup after I stopped a two-on-one Soviet rush [in the semifinal] by deflecting the cross-ice pass and then breaking up ice with John Tonelli and Mike Bossy," analyses Coffey.

"Tonelli got the puck out of the corner, I shot, Bossy tipped it in, we beat the Russians and went on to win the tournament.

"Beating the Islanders and the Soviets within four months [the Oilers had garnered their first Cup in 1984 shortly before the international meet] helped people realize I could get the defencive job done and that I wasn't just a goal-scoring machine."

The last of our Norris Trophy winners is Chicago's **Doug Wilson**. You know him; the man with the big slapshot from the left point. It was that shot that netted Wilson 39 goals and 46 assists for 85 points in 1981–82, the season he was named the NHL's best defenceman.

Drafted by Chicago sixth overall in the 1977 entry draft it is difficult to believe Wilson has been in the NHL that long. Wilson has received little attention in all that time, despite being one of the league's most consistent players although hampered by injury upon injury, and despite his outstanding Norris-winning season.

Doug Wilson is one of those players whose trademark is consistency. And when a player is consistent, putting out superior effort night after night, it's easy for him to be taken for granted en route to being ignored.

But being consistent certainly doesn't bother Doug Wilson. In fact, it's what he strives for.

"You never can tell, but I don't think I'll score 39 goals again," says Wilson, who struck for 22 in 1984–85, has twice been named an NHL All-Star and was selected to the 1984 Canada Cup squad representing Canada. "I know the goals were a big reason I won the Norris, but I was really just as happy with the way I played the next year even though the goals weren't there.

"Lately, I've been playing a lot and I haven't been rushing the puck as much. I've been concentrating on my defence and the defencive part of the game the last few years. It's more important for me to look at the defencive end on our team.

DOUG WILSON

Chicago's Doug Wilson is an excellent all-around defenceman with superior offensive skills. His slapshot from the point is one of the league's best, accounting for a career total of 152 goals.

CRAIG HARTSBURG

Craig Hartsburg, captain of the Minnesota North Stars, is the team's linchpin. Hartsburg serves Minnesota particularly well on the power play, quarterbacking the offense in the opposition's zone.

"The name of our game is consistency. That's what I'm striving for," Wilson explains. "You look at any of the superstars in this league — the Bossys or the Gretzkys and Langways — and consistency is what keeps them there. I don't want to have a great game one night and a bad one the next. I want to reach a high level and stay there."

The only obstacle to that goal — and Wilson belittles his talent, for he truly is one of the League's steadiest performers — has been injury. During his career, Wilson has suffered a fractured skull, a broken jaw, a broken nose, groin pulls and the detection of a hypogylcemic disorder.

In fact, as testament to Wilson's dedication, realise that he won the Norris Trophy in 1981–82 even though he suffered with a broken jaw for a month of that campaign and lost 25 pounds. Wilson has missed some games, but in six NHL seasons, he played at least 73 games of an 80-game schedule, proving his durability.

"On this team," says Denis Savard, Wilson's teammate, "he is the one you can count on to stay the same no matter how things are going. He doesn't get involved in any controversy, he just goes out and plays his game night after night."

The same might be said for the finest defenceman never to win the Norris Trophy, the man originally tabbed as "The Orr Apparent," Boston's **Ray Bourque**.

"He's not Bobby Orr; no one can be and no one ever will be," says Boston general manager Harry Sinden, the man who drafted Bourque eighth overall in 1979 and the man who signed Bourque to a reported multimillion dollar deal that makes Raymond the highest-paid defenceman in the league.

"Ray is just the most gifted player *since* Bobby Orr," Sinden chirps.

"I'll never be Bobby Orr," says Bourque, perhaps more than a little weary with the question, especially after his own outstanding NHL tenure, a term that has included the Calder Trophy as Rookie of the Year and four first-team All-Star berths. Ray's just never won the trophy Orr captured eight consecutive times.

"Sure, I'd like to win it," Bourque candidly admits. "But it's not something I can lose sleep over. People tell you, 'You're the best; you'll win it,' but until you do, it just doesn't mean anything.

"The only goals I have are team goals. That's not just me, that's the way it is here. There's such a thing as knowing what you can do and what you can't. It helps if you realise that and you stay inside your limits. If you try to do too much out there, you end up making mistakes and hurting your team."

Bourque has been helping his team with solid and complete efforts on both ends of the pond ("I'm defence and I take a lot of pride in that," Bourque insists). He has good size and strength, using his five foot eleven, 200-pound frame to thwart opponents in front of the Bruins' net.

RAY BOURQUE

Bruin Ray Bourque, Boston's captain, has always been compared to the immortal Bobby Orr. While their styles are similar and he feels honored by the comparison, he is determined to make history as Ray Bourque—not Bobby Orr Jr.

But, naturally, it is on the other side of the red line that Bourque most usually shines, if only because offense catches more glances than defence. Bourque uses a compact skating stride and laser-like shot from the point to ignite Boston's offense.

In fact, Bourque was Boston's fire and flame in the 1984–85 season, leading the Bruins in scoring with 86 points off 20 goals and 66 assists, while doing his usual job of anchoring the defence.

That's just another indication of how complete a player Bourque is — New York defenceman Barry Beck calls Ray the best in the league. "Ray can do everything," Beck says. "He can lug the puck with the best of them, he can make the good pass and he knows how to defend."

"Really good hockey players stick to the basics of doing everything well, not just some things," Bourque says as he accepts the compliment. "But there are a lot of things I haven't done that I need to do, like getting 100 percent consistency into my game."

When Ray Bourque gets all those things together, the result can only be more bad news for 20 other NHL clubs.

If ever there was an athlete who grew or matured into his status as a premier player, then **Mark Howe** is him.

Howe, the Flyers' superb backliner, came to Philadelphia prior to the start of the 1982–83 season from Hartford in exchange for center Ken Linseman.

Howe had been with Hartford since the Whalers' World Hockey Association days, going to the Insurance City in 1977 along with brother Marty and father Gordie. The three Howes had already played together in Houston of the WHA for four years, playing for the Aeros on a father-son line in a family dream come true.

Mark had always been a quality hockey player, with skills and talent good enough to play for the junior hockey champion Toronto Marlboros and the silver-medal–winning US Olympic team in 1972 — as a 16-year-old.

He went on to become a hero in Houston as the WHA's Rookie of the Year, and a scapegoat in Hartford as the Whalers failed to progress in their beginning NHL seasons.

GORD KLUZAK

Known primarily as a defencive defenceman, Boston's Gord Kluzak has been effective for the Bruins on the power play, where he can use his six foot four, 220-pound frame to advantage by planting himself in front of the opposition net. Kluzak also can move the puck, dishing off for 31 assists in 1985–86.

Things went sour in Hartford after Howe suffered an almost tragic injury, ramming into the steel point that used to be in the base of all goal nets. The stake went through Howe, missing his spinal cord by just an inch. Howe lost 35 pounds during his six-week recuperation but returned to try to lead the Whalers — unsuccessfully — to a playoff berth.

But Whaler management was unsatisfied with Howe's effort and even hinted that he should retire. Instead Howe, who had a no-trade clause in his contract, waived the right and was sent to the Flyers.

"When things went wrong in Hartford," Howe says, "a lot of times the blame seemed to fall on me. Maybe they expected too much out of me. They wanted me to go out and score 100 points [the Whalers had traded 100-point man Mike Rogers and so were looking for an offensive force], but that's tough for a defenceman.

"Looking back, there's no way I should have ever gone back to play when I did. But the team ran into trouble and wanted me to try. When camp opened for the next season I was still under my

MARK HOWE

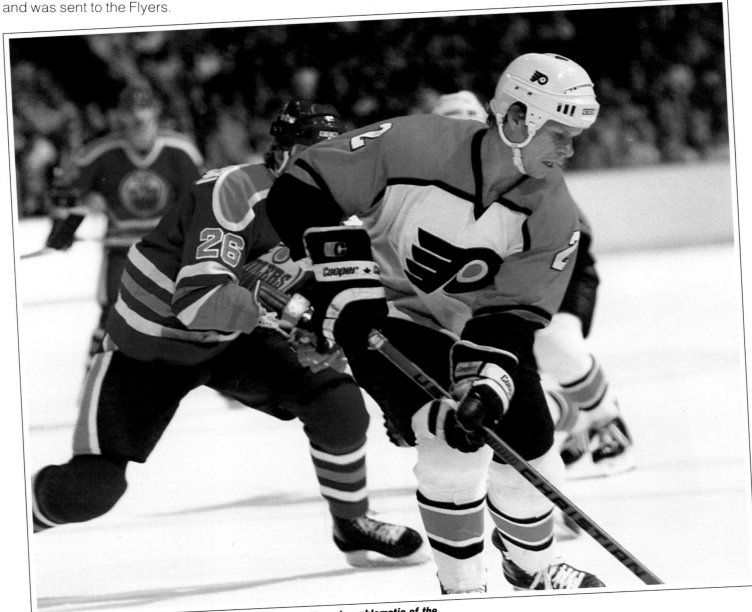

Philadelphia's Mark Howe is emblematic of the "new" Philadelphia Flyers—tough and aggressive, but with speed. Howe has energized the Flyers on the power play with his fine passing and shooting skills.

ROB RAMAGE

Though he has never lived up to his billing as a first-round draft choice, Rob Ramage is an important element of the St. Louis Blues. He too shines on the power play because of his puckhandling ability.

playing weight and I didn't feel right until February, by which time we were mathematically eliminated from the playoffs.

"Management didn't think I was trying, but I didn't have the strength or the stamina I had before the injury. When the Flyers called me at the end of the season, I told them they didn't have to talk me into a trade because Philadelphia was one of the places I wanted to go. The atmosphere here is so great, it's like making another million dollars a year."

And Howe, despite some setbacks in his first season or two with Philly, has been worth a million bucks to the Flyers. "He did everything we expected of him," says Flyer general manager Bob Clarke, who played alongside Howe until his own retirement two seasons back. "Mark gave us something we never had before and that was a guy who could carry the puck out of our end."

"Carrying the puck is my game," Howe says. "I'm not comfortable if I stay back because I feel I have enough speed to get back if I have to. I just think I'm better if I can force the play a little at the other end."

Maybe Mark Howe feels comfortable forcing the play in the opposing zone because he was a forward before being put back on the blue line. For the Buffalo Sabres, **Phil Housley** does the same job as Howe.

Like Howe, Housley has been moved all over the ice by his Sabre bosses in order to maximise his fine skating and offensive talents.

"It keeps me on my toes, I'll say that," says the red-haired, 21-year-old native of St. Paul, Minnesota. "As a defenceman, I have to know when to hang back in my zone and when to rush the puck. At centre you can attack with the puck and if you get caught, there's usually someone to back you up. No one can help you if you get caught as a defenceman."

It was as a centre that Housley had his best statistical success, tallying 31 goals during the 1983–84 season while playing the pivot between Paul Cyr and Mike Foligno.

PHIL HOUSLEY

Buffalo's Phil Housley, shifted between centre and defence by Sabres' GM Scotty Bowman because of his tremendous puckhandling skill, is also a fine skater. Housley was one of the first American players to jump from high school to the NHL.

But perhaps that success did Phil a little more harm than good. Housley was also caught in the inevitable Bobby Orr comparison, some brought on by Phil's coach himself, Scotty Bowman.

"He's the closest thing I've ever seen to Bobby Orr," says the great Scott. "He's not as explosive or conspicuous as Orr was but Phil has the same kind of instincts. Instincts that can't be taught. He's always a step ahead of everyone else.

"Phil has been able to come up with the big plays when we need them," Bowman continues. "But we have to be patient and realise his age. As the team gets better, he may not surface as much as he once did, but I think his evolution has been on target. We think he could be a good penalty-killer, a forward penalty-killer and a good point man on the power play. We think he'll be a good game-breaking type of player because he has a gambling instinct.

"What we're trying to work on now is, when the need is to be safe, Phil fulfills that need."

In other words, Bowman wants Housley to shore up his defensive capabilities. But don't blame Housley; just like any other high-school kid plunked right into the National Hockey League, there were bound to be some things Housley wouldn't do correctly all the time.

"I never had any problems with my offensive abilities," Housley says. "But throughout my first season I kept concentrating on defence and improving my play in that area. I feel I'm getting smarter each time out and I'm not getting caught up-ice as much."

And as for the Bobby Orr comparisons? "It was very nice to be compared to Bobby Orr. But I'm Phil Housley and I want to make a name for myself."

Making a name for himself while making a name for the New York Rangers is super-star **Reijo Ruotsalainen**, a Finnish player called by many NHL observers the best pure skater in the league. Reijo was honoured

Dubbed "the Finnish Wayne Gretzky" for the attention he garners back home, the Rangers' Reijo Ruotsalainen may be the NHL's best—to say nothing of fastest—pure skater. Reijo's booming slapshots have netted him seasons of 20 and 28 goals.

GARY SUTER

Calgary Flames' Gary Suter burst onto the NHL scene in 1985–86, his rookie season. An excellent point-man on the power play, Suter racked up 50 assists in his initial NHL campaign.

for his talents by being selected to the Wales Conference team for the 1986 All-Star game.

Though small (he's only five foot eight and just barely 170 pounds), Reijo is blessed with a fine set of wheels that makes him one of the smoothest and fastest of the NHL's players. The two skating assets, combined with a cannonball of a shot from the blue line, make Ruotsalainen an enormous threat for the sometimes undermanned Rangers.

Billed as the "Wayne Gretzky of Finland," Rexi (as he is called by his Ranger mates) began his hockey career as a young boy.

"I started playing hockey early," Reijo says, "and by the time I was seven or eight years old we were on the ice four or five hours a day every day. My friends and I would just play and play, even after the lights went off.

"My father was my coach and I learned a lot from him. I play though, because it is fun. When I first thought about trying to play hockey in the NHL everyone at home was saying that there is a lot of fighting and that they would try to break me. I just knew that I would have to be a good skater, a fast skater, or I wouldn't even get there."

"I'm not exaggerating when I say that Reijo is the best skater I have ever seen," says Anders Hedberg, a former teammate of Rexi's and now a member of Ranger management — a man who also had a certain reputation as a skater. "Speed, turning, changing direction suddenly, explosive acceleration and balance — he excels in every aspect."

Drafted in the sixth round by the Rangers in 1980, Reijo joined the Rangers for the 1981–82 season and scored his first NHL hat trick on St. Patrick's Day, producing one of New York's lighter sports moments.

After hundreds of green hats were removed from the ice, Ruotsalainen, on the bench, doffed a bowler and bowed to the crowd. Teammate Barry Beck very quickly pulled his little friend back to the bench.

"I told him we don't do that here, not if we don't want to have to worry about ourselves when we get back on the ice," Beck chuckled later. Beck could be especially concerned, for he has been teamed with Reijo for the better part of four seasons.

Ruotsalainen, for his part, has delivered on the promise that convinced Ranger scout Lars Erik Sjoberg to tout him. Reijo has never scored fewer than 56 points per campaign and never played fewer than 74 games. In 1984–85 he was the team leader in points with 73 and assists with 45 and was second in goals with 28. All that, while splitting time between right defence and left wing.

And the goals for this impish veteran? No different, assuredly, than any of the other defencemen across the spectrum we've visited. Says Reijo Ruotsalainen: "I want to be a good, no, a better hockey player."

Goalies

"Where," wail the purists of yesteryear, "are all the great goaltenders? Where are the equals of Bernie Parent and Ken Dryden, of Jacques Plante and Gump Worsley, of Terry Sawchuck and Turk Broda? Where, oh where, have they gone?"

Surprise, fellas. The great puck-stoppers are still here, just under different aliases.

Perhaps more than any other in his fraternity, mostly because he served an eight-year apprenticeship with a sub-par team as it pulled itself up by its bootstraps — and then bore the weight of the club on his shoulders whenever they faltered — the Islanders' **Bill Smith** is a throwback to those legendary goaltenders. During their Stanley Cup championship years of 1980–83, Smith backstopped the Islanders in more playoff games than any other goaltender in history — 129.

Smith set other playoff ecords during the Islanders' reign, most notably for most wins in a playoff year with 15. He did that twice, winning 15 of 20 playoff games in 1980 and winning a spectacular 15 of 18 playoff contests in 1982.

But why is Smith a throwback? Because he is a playoff goaltender and, though his famous predecessors were strong throughout the season, when the playoffs came they carried their teams. So, too, does Smith.

"Just put the money on the table and I'll be there," Smith says. And the evidence backs him up.

Smith has broken many hearts along the playoff trail simply by his refusal to allow another team to score. The evidence is overwhelming: in the opening round of the 1982 playoffs, in the overtime of the deciding fifth game against the Pittsburgh Penguins, Smith rejected shot after shot (most notably a Mike Bullard drive) until John Tonelli could bail the Islanders out with his own OT goal against Michel Dion.

In the same year, in the next series, the Rangers were desperately trying to tie game six, hoping to then go on and force a seventh game. Ranger defenceman Reijo Ruotsalainen streaked toward Smith from the blue line. He met a pass 10 feet away from Smith and in the blink of an eye, fired the puck toward the upper left corner of the net.

Before the missile could break the plane of the goal line, Smith has enveloped it in his catching glove; his save snuffed out the Rangers' hopes.

Fast forward to 1983, the Stanley Cup finals, Islanders versus the Edmonton Oilers. The Oilers are the most powerful offensive team in National Hockey League history. Game One ends, 2–0. Smith has shutout the high-flying Oilers, who never recover and exit the series in four straight games.

In 1984 the foes, once again, are the crosstown rival New York Rangers. Though the Rangers tie the game at 2–2 with just 39 seconds remaining in the third period to force overtime, it is Smith who stars again.

He thwarts Ranger Bob Brooke from dead-on and blunts one Ranger attack after another in the extra session until Ken Morrow can find a way to score and propel the Islanders onward.

"In the years that I've played and coached pro hockey," says Don Cherry, now a commentator for "Hockey Night in Canada," "there's never been a player who's wanted to win as bad as Smitty. That's why you won't find a better money goalie. In the clutch department," adds Cherry, "a case could be made for Smith as the greatest goalie of all time."

"He's the best I've ever seen," says former teammate John Tonelli. "Time and again he comes up big for us with the saves when it counts."

With Smith in what looks to be the twilight of a brilliant career, it is ironic to note that the man who may very well be the best goaltender in the National Hockey League today earned his reputation as a stopper the same way Smith did.

BILL SMITH

The Islander's Bill Smith at his argumentative best. Vilified by many for his excessive use of his stick, Smith is still one of the finest goalies to ever play the game.

GRANT FUHR

Put it this way: Could Edmonton play firewagon hockey if their goaltender wasn't good enough to bail them out? Grant Fuhr, the Oilers' masked man, is simply the league's best.

In 1984, the Edmonton Oilers met the New York Islanders in the Stanley Cup finals for the second straight year. With a continent remembering the year before — when Smitty had blanked the Oilers 2–0 in game one — the Oilers prepared to mount an assault on the Cup.

The final score of Game One in 1984, at the Islanders' Nassau Coliseum home, was 1–0, Edmonton. The architect of that effort was **Grant Fuhr**, MVP of the 1986 All-Star game, a quiet athlete who lets his performance do all the talking.

Fuhr was drafted by the Oilers in 1981, the eighth choice overall and one of the most coveted.

"Barry Fraser, our chief scout, told me the year before that we would take Grant," says Glen Sather, president/general manager/coach of the Edmonton Oilers. "I was a little reluctant, but we stuck with our decision and look what we've got."

What they've got is a goaltender who was named a second-team All Star in 1982, a net-minder with the fastest hands and feet in the NHL, even if he is overlooked because of all of Edmonton's other talent.

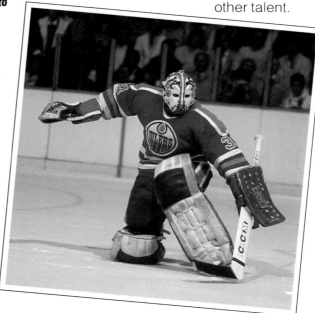

Overlooked is the word that best explains the career of Calgary's **Reggie Lemelin**. Or, as perhaps said better by John Davidson, of "Hockey Night," "Reggie is the Rodney Dangerfield of the National Hockey League. You watch him against the Islanders, he stones 'em," says Davidson. "You watch him against the Bruins, he stones 'em. I get asked by people if he's like that all the time and I tell them yes."

Drafted into the NHL in 1974 by the Philadelphia Flyers, Lemelin signed with Atlanta in 1978 and made the move to Calgary with the Flames. But before the 1984–85 season, Lemelin was always on the outside looking in.

First the Flames had Dan Bouchard. Then Pat Riggin. Then Don Edwards. Then Tim Bernhardt before finally settling on Lemelin, after he had labored in hockey's minor leagues for six years.

Lemelin plays what could be called textbook goal. Reggie is excellent at cutting his angles and waiting for the shooter, never committing himself.

"All I ever wanted was a chance to prove myself," Lemelin says. "You've got to be given a chance to make a mistake and then to correct it and sometimes I didn't get that chance. It just seemed that every year I had to prove myself again and again and it got pretty discouraging."

Well, prove himself he did, and never more so than in the 1984 Canada Cup series when he came off the bench, without any warmup, and thwarted Team Sweden in the final of the series that would clinch the championship for Canada.

There was irony in that too, for the man Lemelin replaced, Pete Peeters, had been the heir apparent for the Flyers while Lemelin was still under contract to the Philadelphia team.

"It wasn't an easy thing to do," Reggie remembers about coming in relief. "You have to be aware that our guys are barely holding on — you have to be aware of that situation — but you also have to keep it out of your mind so you can concentrate and stop the puck. All I could do was go in and play." Which is all he's ever done. That's how Reggie Lemelin got through all the down years before he made it to the big time.

REGGIE LEMELIN

Calgary's Reggie Lemelin is consistently one of the NHL's top netminders. Unfortunately for him, news doesn't seem to travel out of the Canadian west too quickly—and when it does it usually refers to the Edmonton Oilers. But Lemelin is a fine goalie, and here he is aided by former Flame Steve Konroyd in thwarting New Jersey's Greg Adams.

Tom Barrasso, the Sabres young netminder, demonstrated something he knew all along in the 1984 Canada Cup: that he is one of the world's best goalies. Boston's Randy Burridge is stopped on the goal-line by a sprawling Barrasso.

As unheralded as Reggie Lemelin was in his introduction to the NHL, that's how trumpeted was the arrival of Buffalo's **Tom Barrasso**.

As an 18-year-old high-school senior, Barrasso was selected fifth overall in the 1983 entry draft by Buffalo Sabre general manager Scotty Bowman, who thought he saw in his six foot four draft prize the same things he saw in Ken Dryden, the goaltender who led Montreal to four consecutive Stanley Cups in the 1970s, when Bowman was the coach of the Montreal Canadiens.

Barrasso, out of Acton-Boxboro High School near Boston, had already begun attracting scouts when he was a sophomore; by the time of his graduation, the world was at his feet, literally.

Aside from a scholarship offer from Providence University — and the Sabres contract, of course — Barrasso was selected as a goaltender for the 1984 United States Olympic team. The young man had a difficult time making his decision.

"To play professionally has been my goal since I was eight years old," Barrasso says. "I didn't want to hurt the Olympic team by leaving them without a qualified goalie and if I thought I was hurting them, I wouldn't have left."

GLENN RESCH

"If I stayed and I wasn't happy, I wouldn't have been fulfilling my goals," says Barrasso, who has suffered much criticism for what's called his cocky, arrogant attitude — a description probably inspired by such forthright statements as the one above.

"I'm sure some of the fans of the Olympic team didn't understand my decision and I wish I could have done both, but I have to pursue my goals and not those of other people."

Barrasso is flattered by those who compare him with Dryden. The youngster's performances and accomplishments in his rookie year didn't do anything to discourage the comparisons

Tom became only the third goaltender in the history of the league to capture the Calder Trophy as the league's best rookie and the Vezina Trophy as the loop's best goaltender in the same year — his first year out of high school. If Tom Barrasso wants to earn a doctorate, the NHL had better look out.

Traded by the Devils to the Philadelphia Flyers in March of 1986, Chico Resch is one of the NHL's most popular performers, in addition to being one of the loop's best goaltenders.

PATRICK ROY

The Montreal Canadiens were banking on youngster Patrick Roy to backstop them to greatness and he responded, carrying them to the Stanley Cup in 1986. Roy was named playoff MVP for his performance.

MIKE LIUT

Hartford's Mike Liut has long been recognized as a top-notch goaltender. He lived up to his billing during the spring of 1986 when he carried the Whalers in their playoff drive.

There's another goaltender in the NHL who once heard the Ken Dryden comparisons. For a while, **Mike Liut** was truly the franchise.

Playing for the St. Louis Blues, Liut led them to their best season ever in 1980–81, when the Blues finished with 107 points, but lost in the quarterfinals of the playoffs to the New York Rangers.

Tall and rangy, with quick hands and feet, Liut has long been on the threshold of greatness. As he leads another team toward NHL respectability, Liut looks like the game-saver he was in 1980–81.

He stars now for the Hartford Whalers, playing for general manager Emile Francis, who was also Liut's g.m. in St. Louis. Francis, knowing about Mike and his potential, made acquiring the big man a priority two seasons ago.

"Mike is so bright that I swear it rubs off on some of the other guys," cheers Francis, himself once a goaltender in the NHL. "Mike just makes them more intelligent as people and he lifts their self-esteem. He's a winner and a leader and they don't want to disappoint him, so that affects their pride and their confidence."

"Every year I've learned something new about myself," says Liut, a Bowling Green University graduate. "What it takes to play, how to cope with anxiety and setbacks, pressure and success. I think I've matured a lot in the last five years and I probably have about five years left. I'm looking forward to those seasons."

GOALIES

The New York Rangers have a young man tending goal for them now who has the Blue Shirts looking forward to upcoming seasons of success.

A winner at every competitive level, **John Vanbiesbrouck** is giving the New York Rangers goaltending that only the very best in the NHL can match.

"A lot of the guys here were surprised at how well I could perform," Vanbiesbrouck says. "I just told them that they had to see me play two or three games in a row and then they'd know."

Handed the goaltending slot by New York Ranger coach Ted Sator in training camp for the 1985–86 season (veteran Glen Hanlon had been demoted and then reinstated two months into the season), John Vanbiesbrouck ran up numbers that kept him at the top of the goalie stat charts for wins, goals-against average and save percentage.

"Why did he get the job?" asks Sator. "The main reason is John Vanbiesbrouck. He's a quality young man and a fine goaltender."

JOHN VANBIESBROUCK

The New York Rangers have made John Vanbiesbrouck the foundation of their team. Vanbiesbrouck, here watching a shot by Edmonton's Dave Hunter sail wide of the net while former Ranger Steve Richmond defends, won the Vezina Trophy as the NHL's best goaltender for his performances.

MARIO GOSSELIN

Quebec's Mario Gosselin—Goose, to his teammates—proved to be so good when he debuted
with the Nordiques after the 1984 Olympics, that
Quebec was able to trade veteran goaltender Dan
Bouchard to Winnipeg.

BOB FROESE

Philly's Bob Froese responded admirably to the
challenge of carrying the Flyers following the
death of All-Star goaltender Pelle Lindbergh early
in the 1985–86 season. Froese finished that
campaign with the NHL's best goals-against
average and save percentage, as well as the
league lead in shutouts.

Vanbiesbrouck also gives the Rangers something they haven't had for a long time — a young goalie with a big future ahead of him. If his future is anything like his past, Vanbiesbrouck is going to make the Rangers very happy.

As a junior for the Sault Ste. Marie Greyhounds, Vanbiesbrouck allowed the fewest goals in the Ontario Hockey League. When he starred for the Tulsa Oilers in the now-defunct Central Hockey League, Vanbiesbrouck was named that loop's MVP, as well as being named The *Hockey News* Minor League Player of the Year.

"John is just so confident," says teammate Barry Beck. "He's cocky in a positive way I mean, he just wants to get out there and play. No one has to twist his arm to play or practice."

Vanbiesbrouck has good fundamentals, but if you ask him, he'll tell you that mentally is where he needs to improve. "My problem, when things don't go well," he says, "is that I try to do everyone else's job and play everyone else's position. That means I'm paying less attention to what I'm supposed to be doing and that's stopping the puck."

If John Vanbiesbrouck continues stopping the puck the best he knows how and continues to justify the faith that Ranger management placed in him, then the Rangers' future is very rosy indeed.

In fact, if all these netminders continue to perform so admirably, maybe those folks searching for the good old days will realise that they've been right here all along.

Andy Moog makes up the other half of Edmonton's goaltending tandem, giving the Oilers the best 1–2 goalie punch in the league. Oiler coach Glen Sather doesn't hesitate to use one or the other in any situation.

CLINT MALARCHUK

The emergence of Clint Malarchuk, after a five-year stint in the minors, was a pleasant surprise for the Quebec Nordiques. Malarchuk posted four shutouts for Les Nordiques, finishing second behind Bob Froese's five whitewashes in the 1985–86 season.

One of too-few bright spots on a dingy Vancouver Canucks team, goalie Richard Brodeur is once again playing with the authority that crowned him "King Richard" during the Canucks' march to the Stanley Cup finals in 1982.

RICHARD BRODEUR

The Great

He has been the subject of intense media scrutiny since the age of 10, when he scored 378 goals in a season. Since then, **Wayne Gretzky** has dominated hockey in a way that no one has ever dominated any other sport.

Though he seems to grow less spectacular with each passing season, this is only because the perception of his accomplishments has changed. Simply, Wayne Gretzky has spoiled hockey fans.

Gretzky owns or co-owns at least 37 National Hockey League records, spread throughout outstanding regular season, playoff and All-Star game performances; he has been named the NHL's Most Valuable Player for six consecutive years (from 1979–80 through 1984–85).

A glance down his NHL statistics reveals how Gretzky has made the extraordinary ordinary. He revealed his marvelous talent in the 1979–80 season, his first in the NHL after two years in the defunct World Hockey Association.

Gretzky

Wayne Gretzky is the game's most recognizable player.

Gretzky laid the foundation for his nickname — The Great One — during his inaugural NHL campaign, tallying 51 goals and 86 assists for 137 points.

He tied Marcel Dionne for the league's scoring championship but the award went to Dionne, who had scored two more goals. The season was the first and last time Gretzky has not won the NHL scoring title.

Wayne should have won the Rookie of the Year crown for his performance, but a quirk of the rules introduced the summer before his rookie year (to be eligible for Rookie of the Year, according to the Professional Hockey Writer's Association, the group that decides the winner, ''a player cannot have played six or more games in each of any two preceding seasons in any major professional league'') prevented him from capturing the Calder Trophy as the loop's best newcomer.

The hypocrisy of the rule was see-through and must have been disheartening for Gretzky. On the one hand he, along with all the other World Hockey Association players, had been told that their statistics and achievements in the renegade league were not transferable to the NHL,

The Great One and his nesting place.

Gretzky is excellent at finding the open ice.

Wayne is pure determination in the offensive zone.

wiped out as if they had never occurred because the WHA was not considered a major league. Yet on the other hand, Gretzky was told that his play in the WHA disqualified him from winning the Calder Trophy because the WHA *was* a major league.

If the disappointment of losing the Calder Trophy affected Wayne, he never let on. And, as if his entrance into the NHL wasn't explosive enough, in his sophomore season Gretzky took the NHL and shook it to its foundations. The quiet, almost timid 20-year-old ripped the NHL scoring book apart, striking for 55 goals, 109 assists and 164 points over the 80-game haul.

Phil Esposito, a Hall of Famer and the greatest scorer of his day while he played for the Stanley Cup champion Boston Bruins of the early 1970s, had held the League's scoring record, running up 76 goals and an equal number of assists in 1972 for 152 points.

The Great One spots an opening.

Gretzky moves better laterally than anyone else in the game.

As Gretzky tore through the league in that sophomore year, Esposito enjoyed telling a particular story in answer to reporters' questions about his record falling: "I remember my father telling me," Phil would say, "about a kid he was watching playing in the Soo [Sault Ste. Marie, where Esposito grew up]. And my dad would say, 'Phil, there's a kid here who's going to break every record you ever got.' And I'd say, 'Who is that, Pop?' And he'd tell me 'Gretzky. The boy's name is Gretzky.' "

Well, in the 1981–82 season Gretzky proved to Esposito and the rest of the sporting world that they ain't seen nothin' yet. If Gretzky shook the NHL to its foundations in the previous year, this time he pulled the NHL out by its roots and planted it on its collective ear.

Wayne had served notice early in the campaign that the year would be a magical one. After 38 games Wayne had 45 goals, five away from the measuring stick used by experts and fans alike as a guide to a scorer's ability.

That Gretzky would score 50 goals (at that time for the third season in a row) there was no doubt. But suddenly the hockey world was intrigued by Wayne's chase at another mark — 50 goals in 50 games.

Maurice "The Rocket" Richard, legendary right wing of the Montreal Canadiens, had been the first to perform the feat, doing so during the 1944–45 season.

The record stood until 1980–81 when Mike Bossy, the superb right wing for the New York Islanders, tied the record with his 50th goal in his 50th game.

Yet here was Gretzky, off to a fine start in 1981–82 with a chance at Richard. Wayne was cruising along, having scored 35 goals in 34 games, so 50 in 50 was certainly not out of the question. But then Wayne went wild.

In his next four games he scored 10 goals — four in Game 38 against Los Angeles, and two of those were short-handed tallies. So there was Gretzky in Game 39 against the Philadelphia Flyers in Philly on December 30, 1981.

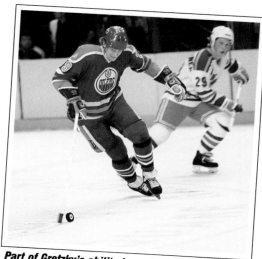

Part of Gretzky's ability is rooted in the balance he has while skating and his ability to control the puck while in any position.

Studying the opposition.

The Oiler superstar wants to repeat this scene come May.

The 50 goals in 50 games was just the beginning for The Great One. Esposito's hallowed record of 76 goals, could Gretzky get that? And 200 points? Hockey people were gasping for air at the thought.

Wayne scored the record-tying goal number 76 against Detroit in Game 63. In the next game, against the Sabres in Buffalo, Gretzky rewrote the record book again.

With the game tied at 3–3 and less than seven minutes remaining, Gretzky wristed a shot under Don Edwards for goal number 77. Gretzky was mobbed by his teammates and later that night by the press — over 300 media representatives from across the continent were at the game.

Phil Esposito was in Buffalo that night, having followed Gretzky from game to game to be there for the occasion. Standing at ice level, Espo presented Wayne with the puck after The Great One broke Phil's record, and announced to the Buffalo crowd, "Thank you, Wayne, for letting me be a part of this."

To punctuate the moment, Gretzky scored two more goals once play resumed, leading Edmonton to a 6–3 win. All that remained was his 200 points.

As with everything else that season, Gretzky's 200-point assault held an air of inevitability. With five games remaining, Gretzky was a point shy, resting on 199 points. Playing the Calgary Flames in Calgary, with his parents in the crowd, Wayne assisted on Pat Hughes's goal for his 200th point of the season.

And to prove he wasn't fooling around, Gretzky got another assist later in the contest and also scored two short-handed goals on the same Flames power-play.

As he had so many times before and so often since, Gretzky made history. He scored five goals in the contest to shatter the standard set by Richard almost 35 years earlier and equalled by Bossy just months previously.

Scoring 92 goals and totalling 212 points in a season that defied imagination, Gretzky was like a test pilot, stretching boundaries until they broke, forcing observers to completely re-orientate themselves to just what good could be.

His 92 goals raised the question of a 100-goal season, something The Great One hopes to accomplish. And his 200 points? Gretzky scored over 200 points twice after that, becoming a standard unto himself.

Of course, the Stanley Cups speak for themselves. Though Wayne was shutout in his first experience in the Stanley Cup finals, as the Islander whipped the Oilers in four straight games, The Great One led Edmonton to two consecutive championships after that, winning the Conn Smythe Trophy as the playoff MVP after the Oilers had won Stanley Cup number two in 1985 by beating the Philadelphia Flyers four games to one.

Little wonder then, that the hockey community expects so much of him and little wonder that he has become hockey's most recognisable personality, eclipsing the popularity of Gordie Howe, Bobby Orr and (the most charismatic of all) Bobby Hull.

But trying to understand the magic that Gretzky weaves is difficult. In fact, novice hockey watchers hardly ever recognize what they are seeing when they watch Wayne play.

Why? Because Wayne is not a spectacular player. He doesn't skate exceptionally fast and he doesn't shoot exceptionally hard. So unless you as an observer know how a play is supposed to develop, you won't understand why Gretzky is so great.

But if you press any expert for an answer, the reply you'll get most often is: "Anticipation." Says Quebec's Peter Stastny, "He has perfect vision and anticipation and he's a great stick-handler. Those talents allow him to accumulate time on the ice and he puts those skills and that extra balloon of time together to do what he does."

Ask another expert how Gretzky does it.

"You watch him out there and he's analysing the play," says Doug Wilson, the Black Hawks' Norris Trophy—winning defenseman.

Wayne's skills are such that he oftens seems to be playing his own game.

Ilkka Sinisalo and the rest of the Flyers know that Gretzky is dangerous behind the net . . .

. . . and now the New York Rangers know it, too.

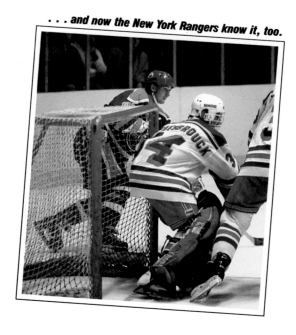

Distance from the goal means nothing to The Great One.

Wayne controls the play from behind the net better than anyone in the league.

"He can see the overall play developing and the entire ice surface, so often he'll make a pass before a man even breaks for an opening and the pass will find the right stick."

Echoes Wilson's Chicago teammate Al Secord, "It's like he's two or three plays ahead of the game."

Perhaps Gretzky is. Think about what Gretzky said in *Time* Magazine on March 18, 1985: "People talk about skating, puck-handling and shooting, but the whole sport is angles and caroms, forgetting the straight direction the puck is going, calculating where it will be diverted, factoring in all the interruptions."

In his book about the Oilers (*The Game of Our Lives*), author Pete Gzowski explains that a Canadian neurologist has conducted tests on sprinters, the results indicating that their nervous systems react faster than those of other people. In essence, they feel the ground faster and are then able to pick up their feet and run faster.

Like baseball's Ted Williams, who always claimed he could see the stitches on any ball pitched to him while he was poised to hit, time must seem to slow down for Gretzky so that he is able to see the play at a slower pace and therefore react to it.

Good as he is, Gretzky is just a part of the Oilers' offensive machine. Here, the Oilers congratulate him after scoring his record-breaking 77th goal against the Buffalo Sabres.

The Great One collects some more silverware.

Gretzky is always focused on the puck.

The Great One has set All Star game records too, and has been named the game's MVP.

If that incredible reaction time is combined with a hockey mind that has practiced and rehearsed each play and can foresee the results of each play (much in the way a chess master thinks moves ahead), then perhaps we have the start of an explanation about Gretzky's magic.

The speed of the game itself allows Gretzky to hide, yet also makes what he does impossible to discern from the stands, unless a fan is familiar and understands at what he is looking.

"It's all practice," Gretzky said in Gzowski's book. "Nine out of ten people think it's instinct and it's not. In my own way I've put in almost as much time studying hockey as a medical student puts in studying medicine."

74

Ready to go to work.

As for his popularity off the ice, experts will say that Gretzky presents a healthy, almost innocent, image. What with positive images of athletes getting harder and harder to find these days, advertisers flock to The Great One in numbers that rival his on-ice point totals.

A Canadian commercial for 7-Up became the first vehicle in the United States to use a hockey player to sell goods down in the lower 48. The commercial starred Wayne and his brother Keith.

In rapid succession, Wayne was representing Canon Cameras, the American Express card, insurance, candy bars, breakfast cereal, and a dozen brands of hockey equipment.

"Wayne catches people's attention because he's exciting and the epitome of the clean-cut North American," says Robert Whicklo, vice president of Traveler's Insurance, Canada. "We wanted Wayne to represent for us the quality and excellence he epitomizes.

"Initially," Whicklo continues, "we were concerned about bringing this young man to professional financial people. But at gatherings, when Wayne opens the door, they swarm him."

Whither Wayne Gretzky? To predict anything regarding The Great One is foolishness bordering on stupidity, for Gretzky's talent is such that it can only measured against itself.

Perhaps we can take hints from Gretzky himself. He believes it is possible to score 100 goals in a season — and he doesn't think he's the only one capable of such a feat, either. But Wayne has said he'd like to be the first to crack the century mark and there isn't much that he will be denied.

The Great One in flight.

Gretzky in a customary pose, this time against a Soviet touring team.

Perhaps he will score 250 or 300 points in a season. Again, in 1984—85, he broke his own record for points in a season. Perhaps he will score more goals in a game than any one has ever done; seven is the record, held by Joe Malone of the 1920 Quebec Bulldogs.

Or maybe Gretzky will score more points in a game than have ever been scored before; Darryl Sittler holds that record, tallying 10 points (six goals, four assists) against the Boston Bruins in 1976.

Maybe Gretzky will lead the Oilers to more consecutive Stanley Cups than ever before accomplished.

But if he were to do nothing else, if he were to retire tomorrow, Wayne Gretzky would still be remembered as the most special player to ever lace on skates. Forget about best or most talented and look simply at how widespread his touch is.

With such as Wayne Gretzky, the temptation is to analyse and study and analyse again. But our demand to understand only short-circuits our ability to enjoy his perfomances both on and off the ice.

Since athletes like Gretzky pass this way infrequently, let's stop talking about how he does the things he does and just enjoy his energy and excellence, as we did with Howe and Hull and Orr.

Contingent

For many years the rule was simple: hockey belonged to the Canadians. The odd American or European could get into the closed lodge of the National Hockey League, but only with great difficulty.

During the early 1960s, for instance, Tommy Williams of the Boston Bruins was the league's only American, and he often paid the price. Many a time he found himself on the wrong end of a collision, merely because he was born on the wrong side of the border.

In the 1970s that experience was echoed by players like the Maple Leafs' Inge Hammarstrom. A Swede, Hammarstrom found himself bounced from pillar to post as Canadian NHLers took runs at him.

Not that anyone ran at Williams or Hammarstrom because they were dirty players or bad guys. The simple fact was, these guys were taking jobs away from Canadian boys, boys who had grown up with hockey in their souls. Hockey *was* Canada and belonged, so the reasoning went, to Canadians.

BOB CARPENTER

Carpenter is undeterred by Rich Preston's position of Devils' advocate.

Well, times have changed for the better in the NHL as more and more non-Canadians are earning spots in the big league. And while Canada remains the premier breeding ground for hockey prospects, it is obvious that the rest of the world is catching up.

Just take a look at Washington's **Bobby Carpenter**. There's no clearer example that the novelty of an American in the NHL ranks has worn off than the youngster from Peabody, Massachusetts.

Carpenter was the most publicized American high-school player in the history of the sport, so much so that an edition of *Sports Illustrated* carried his picture on the cover with the legend, "Can't Miss Kid," while he was still enrolled at St. John's Preparatory School in Danvers, Massachusetts.

When he was selected third overall by the Capitals in the 1981 Entry Draft, it marked the highest place any American had been tabbed to that point. Of course, there were doubters. Could the kid make it in the big league?

PETR KLIMA

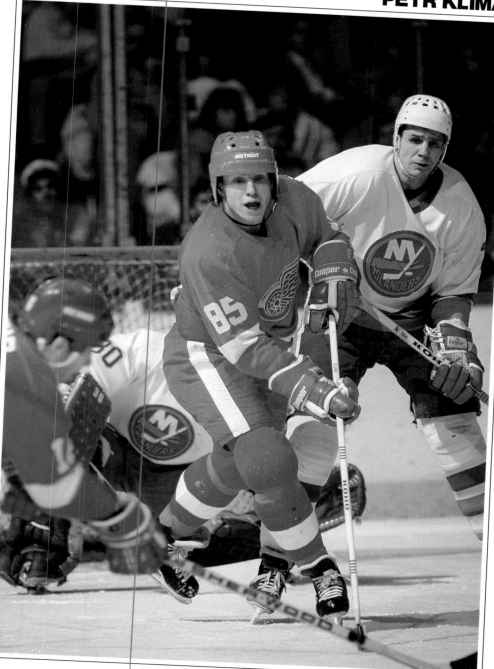

Petr Klima was one of the few bright spots for the Detroit Red Wings during the 1985–86 campaign.

"I'm sure when he came here he felt pressure," says Bryan Murray, the man who took over as Capitals' coach a month into Carpenter's rookie NHL season. "I'm sure everyone felt he could and should be a top player. That's pressure for anyone, especially a high-school kid."

"I wanted to be the first one to jump from high school to the pros," says Carpenter, who was indeed the very first of that breed, followed later by Buffalo's Tom Barrasso and Phil Housley, to name two. "That's not something anyone can ever do again and I wanted to be the one to do it."

Carpenter has done more than just play in the NHL; he has consistently performed as one of the league's very best.

Through the first four years of his NHL career, Carpenter missed not a single game. In year four he performed better than any other American ever, scoring 53 goals — highest ever by a USA national.

"Bobby is an elite type of player," says teammate Rod Langway, himself a New England boy. "He's better than all the Americans in his maneuverability and shooting. He's not Mike Bossy or Denis Savard, but Bobby's the closest an American has come."

Several years before Carpenter scored his 53 goals, the record for goals scored by an American belonged to another fine young centre, one who was a member of the 1980 Miracle-at-Lake-Placid US Olympic hockey team.

Minnesota's **Neal Broten** scored 38 goals during the 1981–82 season, but his success didn't surprise many people, especially not in Minnesota. Broten had starred for the University of Minnesota Gophers, being named the Hobey Baker Award winner (the hockey equivalent to the Heisman Trophy) in that tribute's first presentation.

Broten learned his trade on the streets of Roseau, Minnesota. Not by wearing roller skates (as Calgary's Joe Mullen did on the streets of New York City) but on ice skates, gliding through the frozen roadways.

After his freshman year at U Minn, Broten was selected to the Olympic team, a squad whose success has done much to create the explosion of hockey interest currently underway in the Lower 48. Following the Olympic tournament, Broten returned to school.

With his deceptive speed, superb ice vision and uncanny play-making ability, Neal was an immediate hit in his home state when he joined the North Stars in 1981, becoming a vital force in their drive to that year's Stanley Cup finals.

"When I came to the North Stars there were only three games left in the regular season," Broten recalls. "I just wanted to make sure my man didn't score, to fit in and help the team. We had other guys who would score the goals."

That may be true, but next season it was Broten who scored goals in seven straight North Star games, a Stars' record. Broten also broke the team records for goals, assists and points by a rookie. Yet despite the success, Broten has never developed personal goals regarding, well, goals.

NEAL BROTEN

Minnesota's Neal Broten became the first American player to score over 100 points in the NHL.

"I don't set goals," he says. "I just work hard to play my best every game and if they come, they come. It's very important to use your abilities at the other end of the rink too. If you shut your man down and his line doesn't score, any scoring you do is a bonus."

After a sub-par 1984—85 campaign (just 19 goals in 80 games), Broten rebounded strongly in 1985—86, becoming the first America to tally at least 100 points in a season. "When you have a bad season, it certainly haunts you a little," Neal says.

"It gets to the point where you just don't think things will go right for you that night because they haven't any other night. But it's just one year."

Clearly, the North Stars are going to be picking up a lot more bonuses from Neal Broten.

Another fellow who played on the 1980 Olympic team is the New York Rangers' **Mark Pavelich**. Pavelich and Broten are almost two of a kind. Pavelich, like Broten, has a darting, frenetic skating style, skittering about the ice like an insect.

Pavelich too has fine vision on the ice, skimming passes to teammates that sometimes surprise even them. And he has a goal-scoring touch; witness years of 33 and 37 goals. Durable also: except for the 1984—85 season (when he suffered a broken ankle and missed 32 games), Pavelich missed only six games across his first three NHL seasons.

Yet despite his obvious talent, Pavelich was completely overlooked by the NHL, signing with the Rangers as a free agent in 1981.

Of course, the Rangers did have a skate up on the NHL because Herb Brooks and Craig Patrick (coach and assistant, respectively, of the 1980 Olympic team for which Pavelich had starred) were now running the Rangers — hence Mark's signing in New York.

MARK PAVELICH

Though small in stature, Mark Pavelich is big in heart. Despite his "retirement," many feel he will return to the game he loves.

Mark didn't take long paying dividends in the Big Apple, finishing second in team scoring during his rookie season with 33 goals, 43 assists and 76 points — all team rookie records.

As a sophomore Pavelich accomplished something matched just once in Ranger history, and a feat never performed by an American to that time.

On the night of February 23, 1983, with the Rangers contesting the Hartford Whalers, Pavelich poured in five goals as the Rangers routed Hartford 11–3. His response? "You just have to accept these things."

How anyone could have ignored a player with Pavelich's obvious talents is hard to believe, but the soft-spoken Minnesota native has a suggestion.

"Whenever the scouts talked to me, they were always concerned about my size," Pav explains. "I never thought I'd be given a chance to play in this league. And truthfully, I didn't think I could do it. There was a lot of doubt. My second year wasn't bad and that's where I got to build confidence."

As for his size or lack thereof, suffice to say that Mark Pavelich has yet to back down from anyone in the NHL. "When you're small," he says, "you have to be aggressive or you won't get too far."

The sum total of Mark Pavelich? "It's not just his goal-scoring," says team-mate Barry Beck. "It's the way he fits in and the way the team fits in around him. Pav has a sense of what's going on at all parts of the ice and we need his hockey sense."

Pavelich was the small man who succeeded in the big man's game.

Pavelich left the Rangers late in the 1985–86 campaign, citing philosophical differences with coach Ted Sator. Will Pavelich relent, return to the NHL, and display his skills again? Hockey fans can only hope.

If you're getting the idea that the only good American-born talent is of the offensive variety, perish the thought. The NHL is stocked with quality rearguards of the USA-type, including Red Langway, Ken Morrow of the Islanders and Reed Larson of the Bruins.

Chris Chelios is Montreal's defenceman of the future and already one of the league's best backliners.

But a fine example of the up-and-coming red-white-and-blue defencive talent is playing in Montreal, a sort of American in Canadian Paris if you will.

Reared in San Diego, California (was there ever a less likely hockey breeding ground?), meet **Chris Chelios** — cog in the Canadiens recent resurgence to the top of the NHL.

"As a defenceman in the NHL, it takes three or four years to fully develop your skills," says Langway. "It's going to take time for Chris to develop his style. He's got to learn the moves of opposing forwards, learn to counter them while he's skating backward. There's no doubt Chris has the tools to do that."

An alumnus of the University of Wisconsin hockey team (NCAA champions in 1983) and a member of the US 1984 Olympic squad, Chelios learned the game by playing in a senior league in a southern California rink.

"He's a great player who is super with the puck," says Ed Olczyk, a Chelios teammate on Team USA. "There was no doubt in my mind that he was the defenceman that made our team go."

"There's no doubt he played well against us in the playoffs in 1984," says Islanders coach Al Arbour. "He played outstanding defence against us. With his ability to play defence as well as he does, and with his shot, he's dangerous and should continue to be for years to come."

Not bad for a lad who faced a two-on-one in his first NHL shift and watched the other team score. "I got back to the bench," Chelios recalls, "and [defenceman] Larry Robinson was laughing. Still smiling he turned to me and said, 'Welcome to the NHL, kid.' "

"Playing with Larry in the playoffs that year gave me a lot of confidence, because Montreal showed a lot of trust in me," Chelios continues. "I didn't expect to play the power play, but they put me in there and they had me killing penalties as well. That and playing with Robinson really helped."

And despite the 1985–86 season, a year marred by injury, Chelios has made himself a player to watch for a long time, courtesy of his strong skating and booming blasts from the blue line.

So hockey fans will be singing the praises of these four Yankee Doodle Dandies, and others, for quite some time. Every time they sing the *Star-Spangled Banner*, that is.

Just as Americans have made inroads into the National Hockey League, so too have a number of European players. In fact, on some clubs Europeans are the best players.

Chicago's Ed Olczyk proves you can come home again. He is a native of the Windy City.

ED OLCZYK

Olczyk is a big, strong winger, improving from season to season.

MATS NASLUND

The Canadiens' Mats Naslund. He led the Habs in scoring during the 1985–86 season, tallying 110 points.

"Boy, was he small," recalls Mario Tremblay. "The first time we saw him, we couldn't believe he was going to try to play in the NHL. We talked about him before our first practice and we were convinced he was going to get killed."

Instead, Mats Naslund kills the opposition with terrific speed and hyper-accurate shooting. A Montreal Forum crowd that had chanted "Guy, Guy, Guy," for Guy Lafleur now found itself screaming "Mats, Mats, Mats."

And Naslund found himself leading the Canadiens in scoring for the 1984–85 season, racking up 42 goals and 37 assists for 79 points. He did the same in 1985–86, tallying over 100 points.

"His great skating and puck-handling ability more than make up for his lack of size," says Tremblay. "He has a good head on his shoulders, and he showed an awful lot of heart by going into the corners after the puck."

Tabbed by the Canadiens in the second round of the 1979 draft, Naslund arrived in Montreal for the 1982–83 season, playing that initial season with Tremblay and Pierre Mondou. But injuries forced Mondou to retirement and Tremblay to the sidelines for the 1985–86 season, and Naslund found himself paired with several sets of forwards.

"Even in Sweden I was the small guy," says Naslund with a smile. "But I never shied away from the physical part of the game. I try to count on my speed to keep me out of trouble, but I'll stick my nose in when I feel I can help the team."

For the Vancouver Canucks, a pair of Swedes is doing the same job as Naslund. And out there in the West, the names Patrick Sundstrom and Petri Skriko carry the same weight.

For an example of that, look no further than **Mats Naslund**, also of the Montreal Canadiens.

The diminutive Swede, listed generously at five foot seven, is the catalyst for a team that used to be know as the Flying Frenchmen. Now, with a conglomeration of Swedes, Americans, Czechs and Canadians, Montreal is more like the Flying United Nations.

Patrik Sundstrom, twin brother to the New York Rangers' Peter Sundstrom, has been the Canucks' top pivot for several seasons, squeezing fellow Swede Thomas Gradin from the number-one centre slot.

For three years Patrik has centred for super-scorer Tony Tanti; in 1985–86 Petri Skriko joined that duo to create Vancouver's most effective scoring trio.

First take Patrik Sundstrom. Let's see, the 1980 Entry Draft; wasn't that the year Vancouver drafted Sundstrom 175th overall? Talk about finding buried treasure.

All Sundstrom has done is blossom into one of the game's premier players. In his second year in Vancouver, Sundstrom scored 91 points on 38 goals and 53 assists. To the time, he was the only Canuck to ever score 90 or more points in a single season. And while he has had difficulty repeating his sophomore success, there's no doubt that Patrik Sundstrom is a fine player.

"I know I am a good hockey player," says Sundstrom, "and I never doubted that, not even for a minute. When I arrived in Vancouver I knew it would take time to reach the performance level on the ice that I'm capable of.

"I was prepared mentally and emotionally so I knew I wasn't going to take the NHL by storm. The key for me is not to panic and not to press when I'm on the ice because that would only make things worse. So I relaxed and you saw what happened."

Despite suffering an off-year in 1985–86, Patrik Sundstrom was still the Vancouver Canucks' top centre.

PETRI SKRIKO

Petri Skriko, Sundstrom's linemate, blossomed into a full-fledged star during 1985–86, his first full NHL season. Here he fights off the New York Rangers' Barry Beck, left, and Mike Ridley.

What happened before that soph season was also providence crossed by design. At training camp for that year, he was placed on a line with Tony Tanti. Here were two young men brimming with potential. The two meshed like a fence, Sundstrom floating passes to Tanti and Tanti whipping them, with great frequency, past enemy goaltenders.

"Patrik is the best centre I've ever played with," Tanti says. "He can skate like the wind and he's tough as nails in the corners, a perfect complement to my game."

When **Petri Skriko** was added in the fall of 1985, explosions of the offensive kind started going off. While Skriko and Tanti were machine-gunning goaltenders, Sundstrom was piling up the assists.

Just a little ironic, the success of the trio, for late in his freshman year, while Tanti was slumping, Skriko's play forced his future linemate to the fourth line. Last year the Canucks solved the problem by putting Skriko on the left side of Sundstrom and Tanti.

"Petri's skills are excellent," says Harry Neale, former coach of the Canucks. "He's good defencively and he has great speed. He's a darter. He looks like he's checked, but the next moment he's past a defender.

"Like most youngsters, he's chasing consistency," adds Neale, "and that's especially true of Europeans because they're not used to the NHL's scheduling or the dogfight just to get points. But Petri's a tough little guy and his determination to make it in the NHL will keep him there."

TOMAS SANDSTROM

The New York Rangers have a version of Petri Skriko — a tough guy who can take the tough going. But **Tomas Sandstrom** believes it is better to give than receive, so he gives his share of knocks to the rest of the NHL.

"Tomas does get into his share of trouble, doesn't he?" chuckles Rangers coach Ted Sator.

"Tomas played the same way in Sweden," says Anders Hedberg, a former teammate of Sandstrom's and now a member of Rangers management. "He was a pest and a disturber. The challenge he presents is physical, but not by fighting — you don't even learn how to fight in Sweden. But he makes opponents even more crazy by taking his lumps and then coming back again. That's annoying to people because the respect they are used to isn't there from him."

What there is from him are superb skating skills and an exceptional shot, one that belies his slender upper body. Sandstrom's success during his rookie year of 1984–85 (he led the Rangers in goal-scoring with 29 tallies in 74 games) was a pleasant surprise for a Ranger team that went through a less than pleasant season.

"I guess I did all right," Sandstrom says, conveniently ignoring the fact that he was also named to the NHL's All-Rookie team at right wing. "Playing 80 games wasn't as hard as I thought it might be, but losing so many games and the coach leaving were a surprise to me."

New York's Tomas Sandstrom, here at right being congratulated by Reijo Routsalainen, is an exception to the rule that says Europeans can't be tough.

DAVE CHRISTIAN

Washington's Dave Christian had his best season ever during the 1985–86 campaign, leading the Capitals in scoring with 41 goals and 42 assists.

Things went right for Sandstrom from the opening bell when, appropriately enough, on opening night he scored his first NHL goal to pull the Rangers into a 4–4 tie with Hartford. Sandstrom went on to become the team MVP, as voted by the media.

"His adjustment to the completely new environment that year and his excellent rookie year were things we had to be happy about that season," says general manager Craig Patrick. "He has loads of talent and I definitely think the best is yet to come."

For himself, the subdued young player says, "In Sweden I work as a carpenter from 7 to 4 and then we practice hockey from 6 to 7:30. Here we play hockey without carpentry.

"This is better."

If you listened to Bob Johnson, coach of the Calgary Flames, talk, you might think he too was referring to Sandstrom: "He has good hockey sense and lots of anticipation. He has the European skills, like good balance on his skates, and North American ones as well; he's tough and aggressive and enjoys playing that way. He's going to be a good, complete hockey player and he'll play well in every rink."

But the player Johnson is describing is not Tomas Sandstrom. Rather, the coach is speaking about the "Gretzky of Sweden," Calgary's **Hakan Loob**.

Selected late in the 1980 NHL Entry Draft, Loob had been thoroughly scouted in Sweden by the Flames at a time when the NHL saved its attention for prospects closer to home. After serving an obligatory term in the Swedish army, Loob entered the Swedish Elite League with Farjestad. It was there he earned his nickname.

Loob set Swedish League scoring records by pumping in 42 goals and 34 assists in just 38 games.

"Hockey wasn't a hobby with him," Johnson says, referring to the conditions Tomas Sandstrom mentionec earlier. "Hakan worked very hard in Sweden, so the adjustment to the NHL was made easier for him."

"People say it takes one year [to get accustomed to the NHL], but I don't understand that," says Loob. "Why would you fit in better *after* one year? Why can't you fit in right away? If the team you play for has 25 good guys then there should be no problem."

HAKAN LOOB

Hakan Loob, Calgary's superb right wing, is called a "bona fide scorer" by team coach Bob Johnson.

MARIAN STASTNY

Set adrift by the Quebec Nordiques, Marian Stastny landed with the Toronto Maple Leafs in 1985–86.

"The name doesn't bother me," says Loob who, with his scampering skating style, stick skills and physical demeanor, has been likened to Montreal's Mats Naslund.

"I've been here long enough that people know it isn't true. I won't score 100 goals and I won't get 150 points. I'll just do what I do. I just want to play better than last year."

Flames' management was convinced that Loob would prove his value through the years, so convinced that they made their own Magic Man disappear on Draft Day 1985.

Loob had no problem at all his first year, ringing up 30 goals and 25 assists in his inaugural NHL campaign. In his sophomore year he upped those totals to 37 and 35, respectively.

"The way he plays, we just give him the freedom of the ice," says Johnson. "He's a bona fide scorer on a team that isn't blessed with a lot of natural scorers. His adjustment to the first years in the NHL has been very smooth."

If any pressure accompanies the lofty nickname Hakan earned in his homeland, Loob isn't showing the effects.

Long recognized as one of the league's most talented players, Kent Nilsson plied his trade with limited success for the North Stars in 1985–86.

For years, **Kent Nilsson** was known as Magic to the fans of the Flames in both Calgary and Atlanta, the team's original home. The apellation is not surprising, because for an equal amount of time Nilsson had been called the second-most talented player in the League, next to Wayne Gretzky, of course.

Nilsson made doubters believe their eyes at least twice in his career with the Flames, breaking the 100-point barrier on two occasions and scoring in the 90s twice more. He had 40-, 49- and 46-goal years. This was not the kind of talent you traded away.

On the other hand, listen to Bob Johnson. "He was expendable. We couldn't build our team around him. We tried that, but he never was in shape, wouldn't give a consistent effort or produce consistently. We are going a different route, the honest effort route."

"What do they say about Kent," queried Minnesota general manager Lou Nanne after trading for Nilsson, "Only Wayne Gretzky has more talent?" Nanne would like to see Nilsson, a former Flame, light up the North Stars.

Not that Magic's dismissal was a unanimous decision by the Flames. "He got 99 points last year and was our scoring leader for four of the five years he played here," says Lanny McDonald, the Flames' high-scoring wing. "Where are we going to make up those goals and assists? Everyone has faults, but Kent got things done with the puck."

Nilsson was shipped to Minnesota on June 15, 1985 in exchange for a couple of second-round draft choices. Naturally Lou Nanne, the North Stars' general manager, thought he'd pulled off a steal.

"Maybe they should put an asterisk next to his name: most bad seasons with 100 points," bristles Nanne. "Sure he has deficiencies. If he worked hard every night they wouldn't trade him. But every team has deficiencies.

"What is it they say, only Gretzky has more talent?" Nanne asks rhetorically. "Well, I'm going with talent one more time."

For his part, Nilsson knows he is unpredictable, to say the least. "I know I can look like the best in the world one game and the worst in the world in others. Some games, I'm just not ready. It's probably a mental thing."

"He does have more natural talent than any other Swedish player who has reached the NHL," says the Rangers' Anders Hedberg, a Swede himself and a former teammate of Nilsson's in the World Hockey Association. "When he's flying, Kent can do some of the things that Gretzky does; the behind-the-back pass and the puck through the defenseman's legs."

But regardless of his performances with Minnesota, Nilsson has already made his mark as an import in the NHL.

If a glance at this list of Europeans has given you the idea that only Scandinavians can make the NHL and have an impact, then this next player is for you. A Czecho-slovakian national, Quebec's **Peter Stastny** will stop you from saying "how Swede it is."

Where to start with Peter, that is the question. Do you begin with the fact that he has never scored fewer than 100 points in six full NHL seasons?

How about the fact that he was Rookie of the Year in 1981, based on then NHL records for rookies in terms of assists (70) and points (109) by a newcomer? Does the fact that he is the Nordiques' all-time leading scorer for both the regular season and the playoffs move you?

Maybe you're the adventurous type and like the spy-story quality of how Peter and his brother Anton defected from their native Czechoslovakia?

Well, whichever introduction you prefer, the ending is still the same. Peter Stastny is one fine hockey player.

PETER STASTNY

Quebec's Peter Stastny has never scored fewer than 100 points in an NHL season.

Stastny is often overlooked because he labors for Quebec, a media backwater in terms of communication with the rest of the NHL, due to the club's strong adherence to the French language. Hence Peter's accomplishments, which are reported in Quebec's daily French newspapers, don't always reach the English-speaking world.

Nothing is lost, though, when Stastny is watched on the ice. His passing and skating skills are superlative, as evidenced by his statistics.

"Quebec reminds me of Bratislava," Peter says of his hometown. "They are the same size and I felt right away this is just like Europe and that helped me."

As an example of how comfortable Peter had become in his freshman year in February of 1981 he scored six points against the Vancouver Canucks by scoring the three-goal hat trick and adding three assists.

And if that wasn't enough of a how d'ya do, in the next game, against the Washington Capitals, Peter paced Quebec to a 11–7 victory with four goals and four assists.

Sort of made himself right at home. As have a host of other Europeans who have followed that old-time advice of "Go west, young man." Well, these fellows did. They just had to cross the Atlantic Ocean instead of a continent to get there.

Stastny is the hub of the Nordiques' offensive machine.

The Super Scorers

In life, so the saying goes, only two things are guaranteed: death and taxes.

To turn that around a little bit, in hockey, when you speak of Mike Bossy, Jari Kurri, Tony Tanti, Tim Kerr and Rick Vaive one thing is guaranteed: Goals. Lots of them.

The quintet named above goes under the aegis of the super scorers. These are the players who, no matter how poorly their team performs, will score bushels of goals. And they've proven it.

Take a player like **Mike Bossy**. Since his entrance into the National Hockey League in 1977, Bossy has never scored fewer than 50 goals per season. There are hundreds of players who never score 50 goals in their careers. That's what consistency is all about.

Bossy's is the typical story of a goal scorer. When he was drafted in June of 1977 by Bill Torrey of the New York Islanders, the right wing was the fifteenth selection overall.

The knock on Mike, as it almost always is on any player with such astounding scoring talent, was that he couldn't play defence to save his life. So 14 teams passed on Bossy (interestingly, the crosstown rival New York Rangers had two picks in the first 14 and passed on Bossy both times — only to take two other right wings) before Torrey was willing to try his luck.

Torrey's luck was 53 goals out of Bossy that season. And a rookie goal-scoring record. And a Rookie of the Year award. And a second-team All-Star berth.

Now, almost a decade later, Bossy is a walking awards catalogue: Conn Smythe Trophy as playoff MVP; Lady Byng Trophy for fewest penalty minutes; record for most points in a playoff year (though, naturally, that mark now belongs to Wayne Gretzky); six All-Star team berths; member of four Stanley Cup winning teams.

The NHL gets to see this pose fifty to sixty times a season.

In fact, Bossy has been the most dominating goal-scorer — Gretzky excepted — the NHL has seen since Phil Esposito. Perhaps it is a little tragic that a career as magnificent as Mike Bossy's should coincide and thus be overshadowed by the already legendary career of Wayne Gretzky.

As an example, realise that Mike Bossy has put together the greatest season ever by a right wing in the history of the game. During the 1981–82 season (the year of the Islanders' third Cup victory) Bossy scored 147 points in 80 games on 64 goals and 83 assists. No right wing had ever done better.

It was Mike's misfortune that Wayne Gretzky chose that year to score more points (212) than any man who had ever played the game before.

But it remains obvious to any observer that Mike Bossy is a special player, combining great strength and stamina with uncanny anticipation and physical skill. Listen to Phil Esposito describe the essence of Bossy: "Mike's anticipation and ability to get into scoring position are his foremost assets," Espo says. "There are times when he moves so quickly that he seems to disappear and come up through the ice like a phantom out of nowhere."

"By far the best hands in the world," says teammate Bob Bourne. "The quickness of his release, the way he gets a shot off so quickly is unmatchable. And Mike can take the rough stuff in front of the net. He gets in there and gets mad and then he *must* score."

Says friend and road roommate Bryan Trottier, "Mike has a deep drive, a pride. He's mad at himself if he doesn't score."

"The biggest part of being successful," Bossy explains, "is not being afraid to be successful. I've had the fear that I won't be able to repeat what I've done in the past, but it's never been so bad that it's stopped me. There are people I fear I just can't let down."

Though it is probably that compulsion which drives him, such a fear for Mike Bossy is groundless. And should he choose to retire, as he has planned for several years, the game will miss his style, flair and grace.

GLENN ANDERSON

Usually, just the puck goes into the net when Edmonton's Glenn Anderson scores.

If Bossy serves as the best example of what artistic talent can do, Philadelphia Flyer **Tim Kerr** is on the other end of the goal-scoring spectrum.

As cumbersome as Bossy is graceful, Kerr makes his living the same way Phil Esposito did: he earns it. Not for Kerr are rink-length rushes or blazing slapshots. For Tim Kerr, success is simply standing still.

Or standing in front of an opponent's goal, to be exact. At six foot three and 225 pounds — and with the strength of a moose — Kerr is the original immovable object.

Tim does have one thing in common with Bossy, aside from a proclivity for goal scoring. No one believed in Kerr at first either. Just as Bossy was ignored by 14 teams, Kerr was ignored by 21, eventually signing with the Flyers as a free agent in 1979.

Kerr, if anyone, is the best example of one of hockey's greatest maxims: they never ask how, just how many.

"Tim takes a lot of abuse to get some of his goals," says teammate Dave Poulin, the Flyers' captain, "but he never backs down and he never loses his cool or concentration. He just keeps right on doing his job."

TIM KERR

When he's planted in the slot, Philadelphia's Tim Kerr is hockey's immovable object.

MIKE GARTNER

Mike Gartner, who along with Bob Carpenter is the other half of Washington's "Goal Dust Twins," puts great speed and a blazing shot to work as he terrorizes the NHL's goaltenders.

"I'm not the type of player to skate around five or six guys," says Kerr, in characteristic good humour. "If I skate around one, that's a lot. I realize I have to get in position to use my wrist shot as much as possible, so my biggest thing is a quick release from the slot. I think that's the reason why I'm so accurate."

Accurate to the tune of three consecutive 50-plus goal seasons, despite missing a handful of games in that span.

"He sometimes reminds me of Phil Esposito," says Flyers' coach Mike Keenan. "Tim certainly has the same type of touch from in front of the net."

And, like Esposito, Kerr is difficult to displace from his adopted position face-to-face with the opposition's goaltender.

"It's almost impossible to move him," says Terry Murray, assistant coach of the Patrick Division rival Washington Capitals and a former defenceman. "You lean into him and it's like leaning into a tree."

Somewhere in between the ephemeral Mike Bossy and the all-too-real Tim Kerr lives **Rick Vaive**, a former captain of the Toronto Maple Leafs.

Vaive is one of but seven players to have ever notched three consecutive seasons of 50 or more goals — Phil Esposito, Tim Kerr, Mike Bossy, Wayne Gretzky, Guy Lafleur and Marcel Dionne are the others — so Rick is in some exalted company.

But ask Vaive if his job with the Maple Leafs is to score goals and he'll answer. "I don't believe that a 50-goal season is the sole measure of what I can do for the Toronto Maple Leafs. There are other jobs I have to do, like hitting and checking and working all 200 feet of the rink. As captain, I had to show an example both on and off the ice. I've always wanted to show that hard work can make up for a lot of things."

Vaive has packed a lot of pro hockey into his 27 years. Drafted as an underage junior by the Birmingham Bulls of the World Hockey Association in 1978, Vaive moved to the NHL's Vancouver Canucks in the 1979–80 season.

Vaive played 47 games for Vancouver before being traded to the Maple Leafs, along with Bill Derlago, in what then Leaf general manager Punch Imlach called "One of my best deals."

"Somehow in Vancouver I got a reputation as a bad liver," says Vaive. "It's just not true. I was never as bad as they made me out to be.

Three times a 50-goal scorer, the Maple Leafs' Rick Vaive lets nothing get in his way en route to the goal.

RICK VAIVE

"I thought when I got traded I might have to earn my living as a cornerman, but fortunately, the tough guy period was over by 1980 and the shift to speed was on. I was able to meet both criteria and my toughness doesn't hurt at all."

By the 1981–82 season, Vaive was ready to hurt Leaf opponents with his goal-scoring. He scored 54 goals that year and 51 and 52 in the next two seasons before his production fell to 35 markers in 1984–85. But for a talent like Rick Vaive, it's only a matter of time before he regains his golden scoring touch.

There were those who ridiculed the Canucks after they had disposed of Vaive, voices that loved to talk about how well he was doing in Toronto and how he could have been a star out West.

Though no one in Canucks' management would admit it, someone must have been hearing those voices, for in January of 1983, almost three years after dealing away Vaive, the Canucks mined a little gold of their own.

This was a common scene during Vaive's 50-goal campaigns. Here he occupies the attention of then-New York Rangers Carol Vadnais and goaltender Steve Weeks as Barry Beck tries to wrestle Vaive away from the net.

MIKE BULLARD

The story starts in 1981, when the Chicago Black Hawks drafted a right wing twelfth overall. They gave the right wing exactly three games (over two seasons, no less) to make the club and then traded him to the Canucks.

The winger, of course, is **Tony Tanti** — shipped to Vancouver in exchange for forward Curt Fraser. Now Fraser is doing well for the Hawks, but Tanti has blossomed into a top-shelf NHL gunner.

Tanti scored 45 goals in his first full season with Vancouver and 39 the next year, despite the Canucks' abysmal campaign.

"When we got him," says Roger Neilson, Tanti's former coach in Vancouver and now with the — who else? — Black Hawks, "a few friends of mine called and said how's he doing. I said Tony looked like an alert player but I wondered if he could put the puck in the net.

"My friends said don't worry about that."

They were right. Teamed originally with Patrik Sundstrom and Tiger Williams, Tanti burst from the 1983–84 starting gate with 13 goals in his first 10 games en route to his tally of 45 markers.

The Maltese Falcon (his family hails from Malta) served adequate notice of his hockey potential while a junior player with the Oshawa Generals. He smashed Wayne Gretzky's Ontario Hockey League rookie goal-scoring record by pumping in 81 goals in 67 games, earning Rookie of the Year honors.

Though he does not possess a blazing slapshot, Tanti has an uncanny feel for the net and the ability to move the puck in traffic. Combined with good lateral movement that gets him where he wants to go, Tanti is able to light the red lamp consistently.

"A quick, weak shot is better than a hard one if the goalie isn't ready for it," says Tanti, giving away one of his secrets. Another key to Tanti's success has been the ability of his centre, Patrik Sundstrom, to get him the puck. But Tony's talents are the building blocks of his success.

"He has a knack around the net," says New York Ranger Mark Osborne, a friend of Tanti's. "He certainly isn't as flashy as Gretzky, but when he gets around that net he sure doesn't miss."

"He may not have the hardest shot but as soon as it's on his stick it's on it's way," says junior teammate Mitch Lamoreaux, now in the Pittsburgh organization. "Tony, he doesn't take any time-outs to autograph it."

"I just try to play like Mike Bossy," Tanti says. "That means knowing where the net is without looking, being aware of where it is regardless of where you are on the ice. That's nothing new for me; I've always had a picture in my mind of where the net was."

Pittsburgh's Mike Bullard doesn't miss a trick—or a net—too often.

Vancouver's Tony Tanti idolized Mike Bossy, but it was Wayne Gretzky's scoring record he broke in junior hockey.

Tony Tanti has certainly not had any trouble finding the net. Much like Edmonton's **Jari Kurri**.

Such is life in Gretzkyville — that is, on the Oilers — that some of the world's best players manage to escape view simply by being over-shadowed by The Great One. Were it not for Wayne, Jari Kurri would probably be celebrated as the league's up-and-coming scorer.

Though there have been other Finnish nationals to make their marks on the NHL (Risto Siltanen and Reijo Ruotsalainen come to mind), Kurri is ready to put his own stamp on North America.

Stolen as the 69th choice in the 1980 draft (give all the credit to Edmonton super-scout Barry Fraser), Kurri has increased his offensive out-put every year he's been in the NHL, without sacrificing the defencive part of the game.

He rang up 32 goals in his rookie and sophomore NHL seasons, shifted to 45 in year three, 52 in year four and 71 in year five. Those 71 markers made him the highest goal-scoring right wing in a single season.

Kurri finished off the 1984–85 season with a remarkable playoff, tying Reggie Leach's record for most goals in the playoffs with 19.

"The first couple of seasons were hard for me," Kurri admits. "It's tough for a young player from another country to adjust to things and still play well in the NHL.

"But I was determined to earn a spot on this team and it was made clear to me that my primary role here was to score goals."

Yet Kurri has far from abandoned the defencive end of the ice. In fact, Kurri was runner-up to Bobby Clarke in balloting for the Selke Trophy as the NHL's best defencive forward in 1982–83, and that's after scoring 45 goals.

"He is just a fabulous talent," says Edmonton general manager Glen Sather. "He can score goals, he's a great passer and he's as good defencively as anyone in the league. I don't know what more you could ask for."

"Before we drafted him," Sather continues, "Barry Fraser told me there was no doubt Jari could play for us immediately. It was unbeliev-able we got Jari as late as we did."

Credit Fraser with that. Through his European con-tacts, Fraser knew Kurri was willing to leave Finland, while the other teams had incorrect information. Armed with that knowledge, Fraser simply pulled Jari Kurri out of his hat.

"Other teams knew how good he was," Fraser says, "but were led to believe that he'd already signed a con-tract to stay in Finland to prepare for the world cham-pionships. I was lucky to know he hadn't signed anything."

Edmonton's Jari Kurri, the other half of the Oilers' offensive one-two punch. A Kurri goal has usually been preceded by a Gretzky pass.

Of course, now Kurri is signing big contracts and autographs, earned by his play alongside Wayne Gretzky.

"Hopefully we'll be on the same line for the next 10 or 12 years," says The Great One. "He's the closest in style I've seen to Guy Lafleur. And Jari's covered up for me for years. He makes checking look easy."

About as easy as he makes goal-scoring. That's why Jari Kurri is a super scorer without equal — unless it's Bossy, Kerr, Vaive or Tanti.

JARI KURRI

The Grinders

They aren't glamourous and they don't get a lot of attention, but by doing their jobs well players like John Tonelli (Flames), Kevin Dineen (Whalers), Kirk Muller (Devils) and Don Maloney (Rangers) earn themselves the respect of their teammates and the opposition.

These Chairmen of the Boards come to work every night. On each shift they're hustling and grinding, chasing the puck and getting it to their teammates.

If they were football players they'd be offensive linemen, working in the dirt of the pits, often unnoticed and unappreciated. Unnoticed and unappreciated, that is, by the general public. But to their teammates and the opposition these grinders are the heart and soul of any athletic organization.

"You look at **Don Maloney**," says his New York Ranger teammate, Ron Greschner. "You see him out there working, busting his butt shift after shift and how can you not be inspired? He may not get all the points in the world, but he's one of the most valuable players on this team."

"Donnie used to beg me to throw the puck in his corner," says former Ranger Phil Esposito, the man who used to centre for Maloney on the left wing. "He is just so good at positioning his body, like a guy who pulls down rebounds in basketball, that he can get that puck in the corners."

"By the time I was 16 or 17," Maloney recalls, "everybody started to say that I was good in the corners. I think it was because I kept losing the puck and it was the only thing I could do fairly well.

"It takes a little work," Maloney continues, "but you don't need any great skills to go bashing around the corners and try to kick out the puck. Once they started saying that, I decided I'd better prove it was true."

Maloney, at six foot one and 190 pounds, debuted with the Rangers midway through the 1978–79 season. He was New York's second draft choice in 1978, and his success in the National Hockey League seemed to be a given from his very first big-league appearance.

Premiering against the Boston Bruins in February of 1979, Maloney scored on his very first NHL shot on goal on his very first NHL shift, beating the Bruins' Gilles Gilbert.

The rest of that season followed in magical form for the quiet native of Lindsay, Ontario. Maloney finished with the respectable total of 26 points in his first 28 NHL games, but it was his work in that season's playoffs that proved he was deserving of respect.

As the Rangers charged through the 1979 playoffs to the Stanley Cup finals, Maloney set an NHL rookie scoring record, tallying seven goals and 13 assists for 20 points. Those 13 assists were more than any NHLers in the playoffs.

DON MALONEY

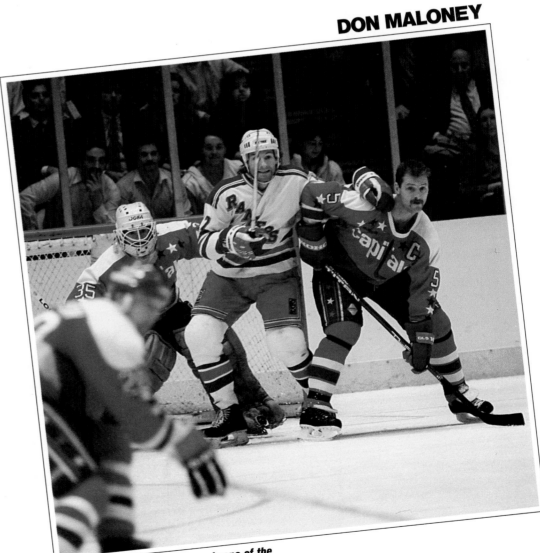

New York Ranger Don Maloney is one of the league's best at grinding in the corners. Here he gets on the nerves of Washington's Rod Langway and goaltender Al Jensen.

John Tonelli, now with the Calgary Flames, long epitomized the spirit of the New York Islanders—work, work, work.

In subsequent seasons, Maloney has scored 29 goals (twice; not bad for a "non-scoring" type of player) and has been twice named to the NHL's mid-season All-Star game. In the 1984 classic, his goal and three assists, as the Wales Conference won 7–6, earned him honours as the game's Most Valuable Player.

Final praise for Maloney comes from crosstown rival Bobby Nystrom, member of the New York Islanders.

"When you play the Rangers, you know the puck will be hard to come by when it's in Maloney's corner," Nystrom says. "I don't know if it's leverage, balance or strength, but the only place you seem to be able to push him is where he wants to go."

If anyone could doubt that Nystrom knows what a good cornerman is, remember that Bobby played with one of the NHL's best, night after night. Calgary Flame **John Tonelli** has always been known as a grinder, a description terribly unfair to his talents. There can be little doubt that Tonelli was eclipsed by the more dynamic exploits of some of his former Islander mates. And that, after all, is most usually the fate of grinders.

But in the Canada Cup competition of 1984, John Tonelli began to garner some of the media attention that had previously been reserved for teammates like Mike Bossy, Bill Smith and Denis Potvin. So outstanding was JT's effort that he was named the tourney's MVP.

"John is without a doubt the hardest worker I have ever seen," Nystrom says, a sentiment echoed by Islanders' coach Al Arbour. "Tonelli will give you 100, no, 150 percent on every shift. He works so hard and just grinds for every goal."

And if that's not enough, listen to Tonelli himself.

"If I'm not out there working as hard as I can, then I'm not going to accomplish anything," Tonelli says. "I don't have all the talent in the world, I can't score like Mike Bossy, so I've got to go out and prove myself game in and game out."

Tonelli turned pro as an underaged free agent with the Houston Aeros of the defunct World Hockey Association in 1975, two years before he was drafted by the Islanders, and perhaps his greatest accomplishment there was to play with Gordie Howe.

After the Aeros folded in 1978, Tonelli joined the Islanders, where his greatest accomplishments are far more numerous. When Bobby Nystrom scored the overtime goal that earned the Islanders their first Stanley Cup, it was Tonelli who made the pass.

When the Islanders needed victories in order to carve out their 15-game NHL-record winning streak, it was Tonelli who got the game-winning goals, including the dramatic game-winner against former Islander mate Glenn Resch. With just 47 seconds remaining in the contest, that goal earned Islanders win number 15.

And, when the Islanders seemed poised to fall over the edge against the Pittsburgh Penguins during the 1982 Stanley Cup playoffs, trailing the Pens 3–2 in the series' final game, it was a John Tonelli goal that forced it into overtime. You'll only need one guess to figure out who scored in that overtime to push the Islanders closer to their third Stanley Cup.

Yeah. John Tonelli.

If Maloney and Tonelli are the old guard of the NHL's digger corps (not that they are finished by any means), then Hartford's Kevin Dineen and New Jersey's Kirk Muller are fine representatives of the NHL's young Turks.

In the months approaching the 1984 NHL Entry Draft, debate raged back and forth over who deserved the nod as the NHL's Number One draft choice. Should **Kirk Muller**, a fine-two way centre from the Guelph Platers of the Ontario Hockey League be the choice, or should it be super-scorer Mario Lemiuex?

The book tells us that the Pittsburgh Penguins, choosing first, tabbed Lemieux, while the New Jersey Devils, in the number-two drafting slot, picked Muller.

New Jersey couldn't have been happier.

"I had no idea how good Muller could be," says Devils' assistant coach Lou Vairo who, as coach of the US Olympic hockey team in 1984, coached against Muller and his Canadian mates. "He was a defensive player playing a solid role on that Olympic squad, so I didn't think he had the abilities offensively that he has.

"Sometimes, it's almost like you might have to shoot him to stop him."

Tonelli is at his best flying down the left wing. Eyed by the Flyers' Dave Poulin, JT looks for a target.

CAM NEELY

Cam Neely—not a flash, but a lot of heart, guts, and hard work. He is now a Bruin.

KIRK MULLER

Muller in his office.

Vairo's high opinion of Muller wasn't the only one. As a rookie, Muller was tabbed by New York Islanders' coach Al Arbour to play in the 1985 All-Star game. Muller was only the second rookie in the history of the franchise (defenseman Barry Beck was the other) to be selected to play in the NHL's mid-season classic; he owns the franchise record for assists in a season.

"I just wanted to come in and progress each year, become better all the time," Muller says. "I never expected to become an All-Star in my first year. I have to give credit to the older guys on the team. There's no jealousy between us."

Jealousy of Muller is one thing that could easily have evolved on the New Jersey squad. After all, from the day of his drafting, Muller was pegged as the saviour and cornerstone of the Devils franchise in its hopes to rise to respectability.

Devils' captain Mel Bridgman, who was drafted number one by the Philadelphia Flyers in 1975, knew what was ahead for Muller and took the 18-year-old (if you'll pardon the expression) under his wing.

"Many times a guy comes in as the number one pick and some guys resent it," says Bridgman, who centred for Muller on left wing early in Muller's rookie season. "Some of those guys have gone through the minor leagues to get to the team and the number one pick hasn't — he's just given a spot. With Kirk, you can't help but like him."

Muller is just as quick to credit Bridgman and veterans like Tim Higgins for helping him adjust to NHL life both on and off the ice.

"It helped me to adjust playing with Mel and Tim," Muller says. "I didn't have to go out and be a hero right from the get-go because I started off with two older players."

In a way, older players also helped Hartford's **Kevin Dineen**. It just so happens that the older players are his brothers and father.

Kevin's father Bill is a hockey Renaissance man. Bill, who currently coaches the Adirondack Red Wings in the American Hockey League, was a player and scout in the NHL as well as a general manager and coach in the defunct World Hockey Association. Kevin's elder brother Gord has been with the New York Islanders for three seasons. Brother Peter labours for Hartford's farm team in Binghamton, New York, and Shawn retired recently after a four-year minor league career.

Ample chances for advice and comfort. And after his very first NHL game, Kevin may have needed all the comfort he could get. With Hartford playing the Montreal Canadiens in the Forum, the Canadiens whipped the Whalers 9–3. Four times when Montreal scored, Dineen was on the ice.

KEVIN DINEEN

Hartford's Kevin Dineen, with is rock 'em, sock 'em style, has become a key man for the Whalers.

"It was wild," Kevin recalls. "Every time I went out there, they scored. I thought to myself, 'Wow, it can't always be this bad.'"

Actually, things improved rapidly for the youngster. Kevin scored 25 goals and added 16 assists in just 57 contests during 1984–85, his rookie NHL season.

The skills Kevin used to put up numbers like those came from high-school hockey in Connecticut, St. Michael's Prep academy in Toronto, the University of Denver and the Canadian Olympic team.

"That year with the Olympic team really brought everything together for him," his father says. But the benefit of that international experience was tempered by some confusion on Kevin's part as to how to handle his future.

"Dad never pushed me," Kevin says, "But he saw that I was pretty confused. He told me that for hockey I wasn't going to get any better in college. I knew he was right and I went with his decision."

Hartford apparently agreed with the elder Dineen's analysis, for the Whalers dispatched one of their most dependable players, right wing Ray Neufeld, to Winnipeg, opening a space on Hartford's number-one line. That space was filled by Kevin Dineen.

"When you think of Kevin Dineen, you think of 100 percent effort," says Ron Francis, Hartford's captain and Dineen's centre. "He knows how to lift us up when we're down, whether it's with a big hit or a big goal."

"I know playing with Ronnie is a great chance for me," says Dineen. "I just keep thinking, 'Don't blow this, Kevin,' because if I play well with Ron I can really establish myself."

In one of sports better ironies, it was father Bill who was responsible for bringing Kevin to Hartford. While employed by the Whalers as a scout, Bill was responsible for Hartford's drafting Kevin.

"Yes, it was a little awkward or uncomfortable," Bill Dineen says. "I never had a doubt in my mind that Kevin could play, but it's still a case of a father talking about his son."

Dineen left Hartford for his current position in the Red Wings' organisation before Kevin came aboard with the Whalers in December of 1984. The way Kevin has played, no one can ever say Bill Dineen did Hartford an injustice.

New Jersey's Mel Bridgman, no Capser Mil-
quetoast himself, gives North Star Ed Hospodar a
taste of his own medicine.

They have faces only a mother could love. At least that's the opinion of the rest of the National Hockey League.

But if you asked Ed Hospodar, Behn Wilson, Dave Semenko, Chris Nilan and Tiger Williams, they'd tell you that rest of the NHL is a bunch of crybaby, mewling momma's boys.

These five, though by no means alone, are members of a small and select NHL group — The Tough Guys.

Hockey has always had tough guys, though names for them have been less consistent than their appearance. Goon is a word often used to describe a tough guy, as are policeman and enforcer. Hockey people will tell you that there are slim differences to be discerned among those three descriptions, but sometimes the differences are hard to find.

In their times, Eddie Shore (Boston Bruins, 1930s), Ted Lindsay (Detroit Red Wings, 1950s) and John Ferguson (Montreal Canadiens, 1960s) were all considered tough guys.

Tough Guys

But they take a back seat to the man who put tough guy-ism on the map, **Dave Schultz** of the Philadelphia Flyers. During the Flyers' Stanley Cup years of 1974 and 1975, physical and often violent (read goon) hockey was the order of the day.

Schultz racked up a record 472 minutes in penalties during the Flyers' second run to the Stanley Cup. To get an idea of how much time that is, Schultz, who played in all 80 regular season games, actually missed almost eight complete hockey games by being penalised.

Paul Baxter, who is second on that list, once collected 407 minutes in a season — more than a full game behind Schultz in our informal statistic. Schultz, by the way, is third on the list, with just 405 minutes.

It was from Schultz's impact that the terms goon, policeman and enforcer developed. Schultz, known as the Hammer because of his exploits, was labeled a goon — though in fairness to him, he fought with his fists and not with his stick, the usual determining factor in goon-ness.

DAVE SCHULTZ

He was the most hated man in the league during the mid-70s, but Dave Schultz was just as important to the Flyers as Bobby Clarke and Bernie Parent.

But the goon begat the policeman, the player responsible for making sure there wasn't any trouble. The enforcer's role was to be on the ice, along with his team's best player, in order to protect the superstar from the goon.

For the Edmonton Oilers, **Dave Semenko** serves such a purpose. Though he can play hockey, Semenko's role has almost completely evolved into that of the enforcer.

When Oiler superstar Wayne Gretzky is trifled with, rest assured that Dave Semenko will be the next player off the bench on a search and destroy mission. Semenko's presence is given by Wayne's detractors as one reason why The Great One isn't so great. They claim that Wayne can't take a hit, even a legitimate check.

DAVE SEMENKO

Edmonton's Dave Semenko, doing what comes naturally to the Islanders' Duane Sutter.

One of the players Semenko has been commissioned to protect his buddies from is **Ed Hospodar** of the Minnesota North Stars.

Drafted by the New York Rangers in 1979, Ed made it to New York for 20 games in the 1979–80 season, playing here and there as a defenceman or winger. He was a tough cookie while with New York but, unfortunately for him, one night he met a tougher cookie — Clark Gillies of the New York Islanders.

The two got together for a little dance, the result of which was Hospodar having his jaw wired shut for six weeks, courtesy of a Gillies punch.

Ed was traded by the Rangers to the Whalers just prior to the start of the season in 1982, so Hospodar plied his trade in Hartford. That is to say, he introduced opposing players to his elbows. Once, after the whistle had blown, he knocked down New Jersey defenceman Ken Daneyko, resulting in a broken ankle for the Devil.

From Hartford, Boxcar (as he is called by his teammates) went south to Philadelphia, a team notorious for its physical play

Ed's highlight film there would include the dental work he did on Edmonton's

Hospodar got his nickname—Boxcar—because that's how he hits: like a freight train.

Mark Napier during the 1985 Stanley Cup finals, removing a handful of Napier's teeth with — surprise — an elbow.

That assault prompted Edmonton general manager Glen Sather to fume, "If the League doesn't take care of Hospodar, we will. And they'll need two boxes for him, one for his head and one for the rest of him."

"He has skills, too," says former teammate Mike Bloski, a goaltender who played with the Flyers after the death of goalie Pelle Lindbergh in late 1985. "You forget that because Boxcar is so willing to go out and stick his nose in and get involved. That's why he can play in the National Hockey League, because he can play hockey."

Traded to Minnesota in the middle of the 1985–86 season, Hospodar is a disturber on the ice, but a warm, compassionate man off it. The Bowling Green, Ohio, resident is a frequent visitor to the children's wards of hospitals in whatever city he happens to be calling home. He has signed again with the Philadelphia Flyers for the 1986–87 season.

The Philadelphia Flyers had another ruffian once (they do seem to specialize in them, don't they?) by the name of **Behn Wilson**.

Wilson, who once fancied becoming an actor after hockey, put on one of his most notorious performances the night he speared the Rangers' Reijo Ruotsalainen in the face, missing the Finn's eye by scant millimetres.

"I expect to be tested," said Wilson at the press conference held by the Flyers to introduce him in 1978. "The other teams will send their toughest guy at me and I'll beat him and then they'll leave me alone. Then I'll settle down and play hockey."

If only. Wilson has demonstrated good defencive talent during his NHL tenure: an ability to rush the puck, strength in front of the net and a good shot from the point.

"I think that corner work is one of the best aspects of my game," he says, "and it's the one that's seldom talked about." Perhaps that's because Behn has had only one NHL season with less than 100 minutes in penalties; he's accumulated over 1,200 career minutes in the sin bin.

BEHN WILSON

Chicago's Behn Wilson, using his stick for that which it was intended. This time.

TIGER WILLIAMS

Tiger Williams, the most penalized man in NHL history. Note the battle scar above his left eye as the Tiger goes on a seek-and-destroy mission.

But Wilson only has a rental in the penalty box. That piece of real estate is owned lock, stock and barrel by Los Angeles King **Dave Williams**, known as Tiger to friend and foe alike. Williams makes Dave Schultz look like a choirboy.

Including playoffs, Schultz finished his NHL career with 2,706 minutes in the penalty box. Entering the 1985–86 season, Williams already had *3,620* career minutes. Tiger has actually spent more time in the penalty box than some men have spent in the entire league.

Williams has been in the National Hockey League since the 1974–75 season and it would be a lie to say that his whole career has been one long brawl. He's had years of 21, 22, 19 and 19 goals scored and while with the Vancouver Canucks in 1980–81 had his best goal total ever with 35.

"There will always be a place for a Dave Williams in hockey," says Tiger. "These guys who are scoring 4,000 goals and criticising fighting are, well, hypocrites. They all have protection. The kids are bigger, faster, they skate better, they eat their granola and they all look like mooses.

"But that isn't the whole story. There are some things they can't do and never will be able to do."

"The value of the Tiger is that he won't let you down," says Roger Neilson who, though now a coach with the Black Hawks, coached Williams in Vancouver. "You can give him a job and he'll do it."

While Williams, now in his early 30s, is in the twilight of his NHL career, another disturber of almost guaranteed epic proportions is on the horizon and moving closer.

His name is **Chris Nilan**, but don't say it too loud in Boston. Surprising, since Nilan is a native of the Hub. Not so surprising when you realize that Nilan plays for Boston's arch-rivals, the Montreal Canadiens, and less surprising if you know that in 1985–86 he butt-ended Bruin Rick Middleton in the mouth to the tune of lost teeth.

In case you're wondering whether or not Nilan was being a bully or just paying back an old evil, consider this: Nilan has compiled more penalty minutes in seven of his eight seasons than Middleton has in his entire career.

Nuff said?

CHRIS NILAN

Montreal's Chris Nilan discusses the weather with Philadelphia's Brad Marsh.

Quebec's Dale Hunter in one of his more innocent moments. He has played every game but three of every season of his NHL career. He missed those three with a league suspension.

Well, not really. Nilan, like Hospodar and Williams and Wilson, has the ability to play in the NHL. He is an effective checker and solid defensive forward. It's just that he prefers to do things like punch Toronto Maple Leaf Rick Vaive.

Of itself, that's not a sin, especially in the National Hockey League where fighting is permissible. Only thing is, Vaive was in the hallway of the Montreal Forum one day during the 1984 Canada Cup when Nilan took his poke at him.

Then there was the time that Nilan and Paul Baxter were sent to their respective penalty boxes after a little bit of mischief. In Nilan's penalty box was the bucket of spare pucks for game use; Chris helped himself to one and then flung it at Baxter.

Just another day at the office for one of the toughest guys in the National Hockey League. But don't you get the distinct feeling that maybe just a little too much emphasis is being placed on the actions of these fellows? That they're no different from the general population? That deep down they must be truly penitent for the heinous acts they've committed?

Naaaah.

The Refs

They are cursed at, spat upon and punched out. And that's just on the good nights.

They are a minority of 40, but any hockey fan will tell you that the men in the convict-striped black-and-white of the National Hockey League's officiating staff have won more games for the *other* team than the opposing squad itself.

Why do they do it? What moves a man to devote 20 years of his life to a profession that has him travelling over 100,000 miles a year, skating over five miles a night, being punched in the head or drenched with beer? A profession that has him receiving death threats?

Surely, to officiate hockey on the professional level requires certain traits, not the least of which is to heed the advice of a former NHL ref and member of the Hockey Hall of Fame, the late Mickey Ion: "Remember," he would tell his linesmen, "from the time the first puck is dropped to the time the last buzzer sounds, the three of us are the only sane ones in the building."

"Why?" echoes Gord Broseker, one of the NHL's 21 linesmen. "It's like any-thing else. You get up in the morning, you look in the mirror and you say, 'I did a good job last night.' You get a personal satisfaction from it."

Broseker has been getting that satisfaction for more than 13 years in the NHL. He worked his 800th NHL game midway through the 1985–86 season and is fairly typical of most of the NHL's officiating staff. That is to say, he works hard, travels hard and gets little credit for the part he plays in games viewed by millions of people annually.

GORD BROSEKER

Linesman Gord Broseker drops in on the New York Rangers.

RAY SCAPINELLO

Ray Scapinello does a little house-cleaning after an Islander hat trick.

JOHN D'AMICO

John D'Amico is the NHL's senior linesman, with over 20 years of big-league experience. He is often called the best linesman in the league by the players themselves.

For better or worse, that has been the law of officiating since athletes began playing games for money: an official's job is to be seen and not heard — and not even seen, either. After all, as the refereeing saying goes, "If you do a good job, you shouldn't get noticed."

"We're in law enforcement," says Broseker. "Same as a policeman. There are rules to enforce. But if you don't apply good common sense, then there's nothing there. The rule book would be nothing without common sense."

Hockey officiating has gone through stages, just as the game has, but the common-sense dictum has remained the same. In the sport's early days, referees used bells instead of whistles to signal for a play stoppage. Why bells? Because they didn't freeze to your lips when you tried to blow them — after all, hockey was played outdoors in its pioneer days. Used to get a bit cold out there, so the refs used a different kind of common sense, you might say.

Up until the 1940s and 1950s, a referee's uniform consisted of a pair of black pants, a button-down shirt, a sweater and a tie. Yes, they used whistles by then. But really, how could anyone *not* be noticed skating around the ice in a sweater and tie, ringing a bell?

Still, referees have been responsible for some of the game's important developments. The first of hockey's great referees was a fellow named Fred C. Waghorne, now a hockey Hall of Famer.

Before Fred, officials used to place the puck on the ice, move each center's stick blade next to the puck by hand, back up and declare, "Play!" The injuries to an official's hands, feet and shins were legion.

JIM CHRISTISON

Christison hauls the puck to centre ice after the Los Angeles Kings give up a goal. Even though play is stopped, the concentration is evident.

RON WICKS

Referee Ron Wicks chairs this zebra convention.

As linesmen John D'Amico and Ray Scapinello separate the combatants, referee Bob Myers is watchful for any further wrongdoing.

But Waghorne had a better idea; he would step a bit away from the players, toss in the puck and get a head start on his hasty retreat. Courtesy of old Fred, the faceoff was introduced to the game.

And, for the record, it was Waghorne who introduced the use of the bell. Another Hall of Fame zebra, Bill Chadwick, was responsible for the use of hand signals to communicate penalties. Why? "I didn't know what to do with my hands," he once explained.

Unfortunate, but just as legendary, are tales like the one referee Red Storey told

shortly *after* he quit about what an NHL team owner said to him shortly *before* he quit. As the tale goes, the owner berated Storey, finishing with the immortal line: "By God, we own this league and you'll referee it the way we tell you to!"

Sigh. Abuse from the top Abuse from the side. Truly a no-win situation for any official.

"That's true," says Broseker. "Half the time I'm wrong, even when I'm 100 percent right. The team that doesn't get the call never believes it's the right one. The replay can back you up, but you're still wrong."

Perhaps that's why the NHL looks for men with guts to handle the men with sticks.

"Above all, we look for strong character and confidence," says John McCauley, the NHL's assistant director of officiating and a former NHL referee himself.

McCauley's career was almost ended after he was punched in the eye by an irate fan — after a game he *didn't* work — and suffered double vision. Though surgery corrected his vision, and McCauley did work once again on NHL ice, the league's hierarchy offered McCauley the assistantship. He knows whereof he speaks.

"And," he continues, "more so today than before, we look for skating ability, of course. We're very specific about that, and about what we want in terms of mechanics, signalling and positioning. Officials have got to give themselves a clear view of the play. To do that, we want to see those referees 10 to 12 feet off the side boards and about 18 to 20 feet behind the play, where they have most of what's going on in front of them. With play around the net, we want them on the goal-line six to eight feet from the net. That's most important."

One of McCauley's responsibilities involves watching officials work in game situations in order to judge and correct an official's mechanics if necessary. He's not alone in that; the NHL has a staff of officiating supervisors who watch all of the league's striped men perform.

The game does have its lighter moments for officials, though almost always the funny moments come from some sort of controversy. For example, there was the time Toe Blake, coach of the Montreal Canadiens, growled disgustedly at a two-minute penalty assessed his team by Mickey Ion.

PAT DAPUZZO

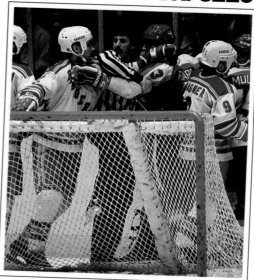

Linesman Pat Dapuzzo gives an earful to New York defenceman Tom Laidlaw after the Ranger cuffed Robert Picard.

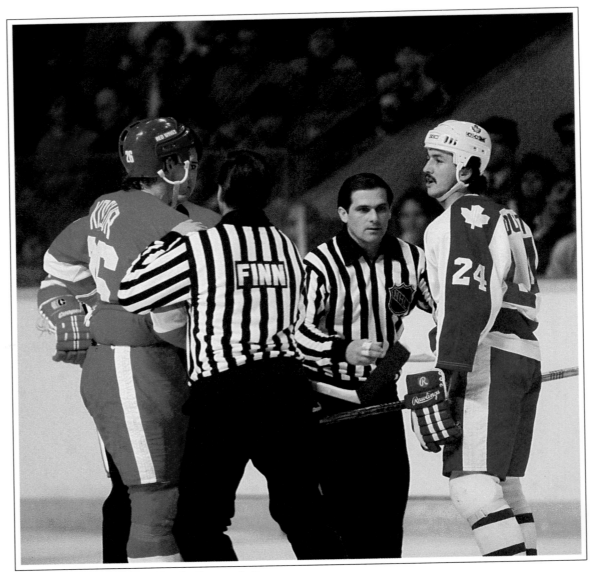

Linesmen Ron Finn and Ray Scapinello move in to head off Detroit's Joey Kocur and Toronto's Dan Daoust.

From the time of the opening whistle to the closing buzzer, the referee and his linesmen are the only sane men in the house. Referee Ron Wicks takes a breather at centre ice.

"You can't guess what I'm thinking, Mickey," Blake snapped at Ion. "No, I can't," replied Ion, as he changed the penalty to a five-minute major, "But no one is going to think obscenities like that about me."

Or the time King Clancy, an All-Star defenseman in the early days of the Maple Leafs and later a referee, officiated a game while a doctor friend was seated at rinkside. All night long the doctor tore into Clancy until finally, tired of the abuse, Clancy skated to the boards.

"You know, Doc," Clancy said, "I sure make a lot of mistakes."

"I know, I know," chuckled the doctor.

"But there's one thing about my mistakes, Doc."

"Oh, yes?"

"I don't bury mine."

To Chadwick, who refereed though blind in his right eye, the fans would yell: "Nice game, Bill. Now try the next period with your good eye!" And every ref has heard, "Hey, you're the second-best ref in the league — everyone else is tied for first!"

But they do get their revenge, the zebras do. A favorite trick, as told by an NHL linesmen, is particularly effective with younger, less-experienced players — though it is said to work with vets too.

"When you whistle 'em," the linesman says, "they always want to know who's offside. So the first kid skates up and demands: 'Who was offside?'

"I'll say, 'You were.' They'll say, 'Me? No way!' So I'll say, 'Okay, you *weren't* offside.' Then they'll skate away and the next one comes over.

'Who was offside?'
'You were.'
'Me? No way!'
'Okay, you weren't offside.'
Then the third one . . ."

And so on.

A sense of humour is almost mandatory in a profession where the stress, both physical and mental, is severe. If not, Andy Van Hellemond (who has been spat at and punched by NHLers themselves) and Kerry Fraser (who received a death threat while he worked the 1985 playoffs) would never be able to perform again.

"Those are things you can't think about when you work," says Broseker. "It's like an occupational hazard, I guess. If it's gonna happen, it's gonna happen. So I don't even let it enter my mind. If I do, I won't be able to do my job and that's of the utmost importance."

A strange occupation, surely. But the officials lucky enough and skilled enough to work with the best players in the world do so by choice. Most officials have other businesses they tend during the off-season, businesses that could support them year-round. For example, one is a real-estate agent, another runs a landscaping business.

Broseker, for his part, was in the Texas Rangers' baseball organisation before accepting his father's invitation to an American Hockey League officials' training camp back in the early 1970s.

"When I started, I never thought I'd be doing it for 13 years," Gord says. "My dad worked part-time in the American League and I'd just come home from finishing the season. Back then, in the American League, they used to have part-time officials in each city and the officials who were working with my dad in Baltimore had retired.

"So I came home and he said to me, 'We're having training camp in Hershey, why don't you go up?' I'd worked kids' games, so I went up there and to make a long story short — Richmond and Tidewater had come into the league at that time and they had no one in the south, so they made me a pretty good offer, since I was the closest one able to travel, and I worked over 80 games part-time that year.

WILL NORRIS

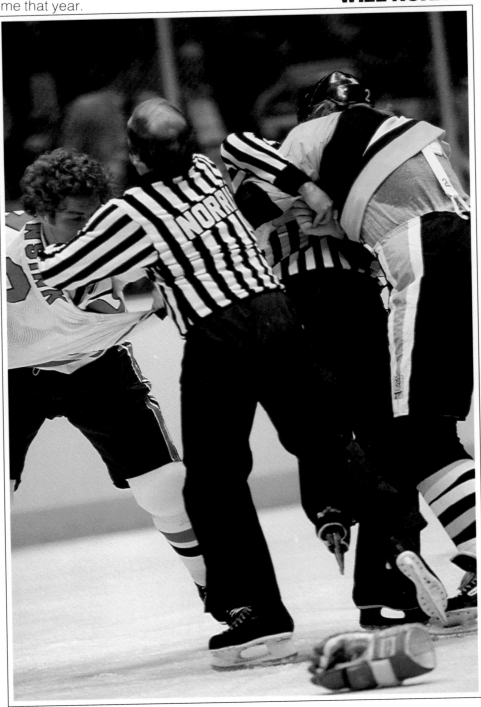

Will Norris gets a hand breaking up this battle. Often, the linesmen catch more punches than the fighters.

Referee Bruce Hood, now retired, conducts a stick measurement as linesman Leon Stickle looks on.

"As it turned out, I got into a contract dispute with baseball — they wanted to cut my salary and I said no — and Texas released me and the NHL signed me."

More than 13 years later, Broseker has become one of the league's more senior officials. The game is not always fun for him now, and that's a change from the old days, but there are still some games for which he can get excited.

"When I was young, I used to get kind of, 'Oh, wow, here I am,'" Broseker says. "That wears off; it has to or else you can't do your job. But I can't get up for 80 games a year. If I did, I wouldn't last the season.

"Just like the players, you can't approach each game like it's the playoffs," he continues. "For big games I get psyched up the night before, I begin to think about it. Sometimes I get so wound up I can't sleep the night before. But if I did that all season I'd be useless at the end of the year. If I were excited for 80 games, I could forget about the playoffs. I'd be so mentally drained, I'd never make it."

Even keel is the key to officiating in the National Hockey League — not too high and not too low. Consistency, just as it is for the players, is the way to work in the NHL, the only way.

It has to be that way. To quote Gord Broseker paraphrasing Gilbert and Sullivan, "Morning to noon and sun to sun, a zebra's work is never done."

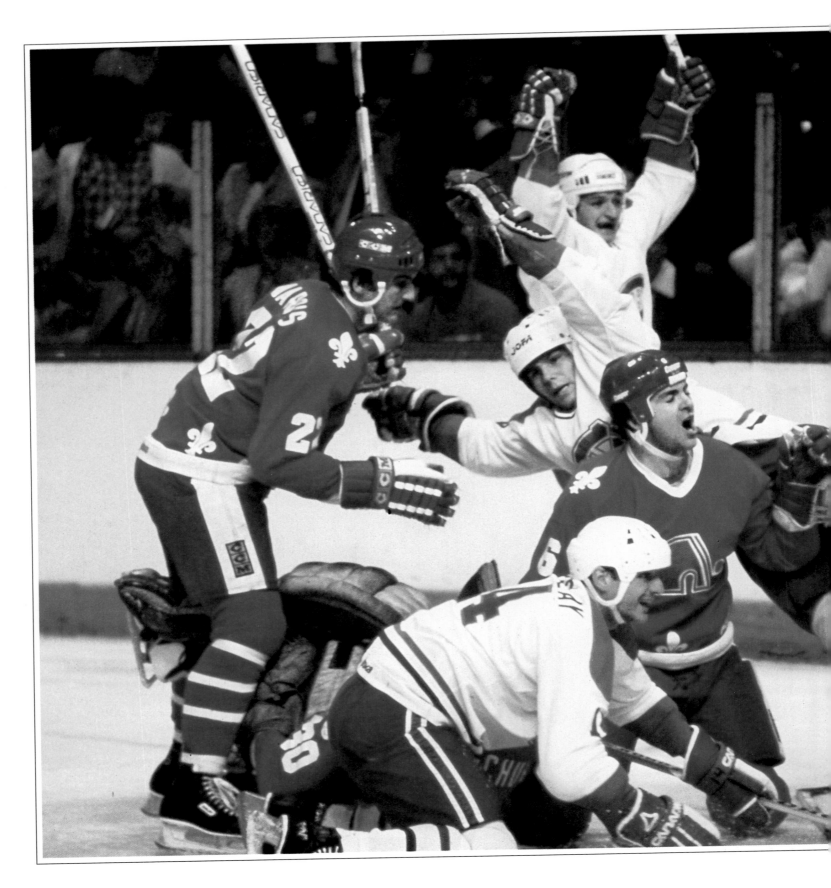

The thrill of victory in sports comes from one thing and one thing only: winning.

There are ways, however, to make that thrill just a little sweeter. Defeating a hated opponent, for example. Or winning for the first time. Or winning when no one gave a thought to your coming close.

Hockey is a history of rivalries, created no doubt by the closeness of the National Hockey League in its earlier days. From the late 1920s to the late 1960s, hockey operated with a small band of teams, sometimes as few as six, sometimes more.

But from World War II until 1967, the NHL had just six teams — the Original Six, as they came to be called. The Boston Bruins, Toronto Maple Leafs, Montreal Canadiens, Detroit Red Wings, Chicago Black Hawks and New York Rangers did icy battle then, and battle it was.

In that simpler hockey era, teams faced each other upward of 10 times a season, rather than the three times most of the 21 teams see each other today. So you were more likely to remember that cheap shot — and more likely to return it — in the good old days.

The Thrill of Victory

The Montreal Canadiens celebrate the thrill of victory, this time a playoff win against the Quebec Nordiques.

Toronto and Detroit, for example, were fierce rivals during the late 1940s and early 1950s. The seeds were planted in 1942 when, during the Stanley Cup finals, heavily favoured Toronto lost three straight games in the finals.

No team had ever lost three straight games in the best-of-seven finals, but the Leafs found themselves in that fourth game, rallied and won the Cup. Game Four distinguished itself not just for the Leaf rally, but for Detroit coach Jack Adams's tantrum.

So incensed was Adams that, with the Red Wings hopelessly behind in game four, he flung himself over the boards to challenge the decisions of referee Mel Harwood. Adams punctuated his arguments with several punches and, after he was pulled off Harwood, found himself suspended for the duration of the playoffs by NHL president Frank Calder.

The Leafs continued their miracle comeback and captured the Stanley Cup, much to the bitter disappointment of Red Wing supporters, who maintained that Adams's punishment was unjust and had cost Detroit the Stanley Cup.

Thus is a rivalry born. Many more series, often bloody and riotous, were played between these two teams. Tempers ran so high that fines and suspensions were more often the topic of the day-after chatter than was the game itself.

Just in case anyone forgot how much these two teams dislike each other, the reminders were evident during the 1984—85 season when Detroit coach Brad Park sent his players off the bench during a game with the Leafs to brawl. Park was suspended and fined for his actions. Just like the good old days.

When long-time rivals Toronto and Detroit get together, sparks fly. Here, Leaf Wendel Clark introduces himself to Billy Carroll.

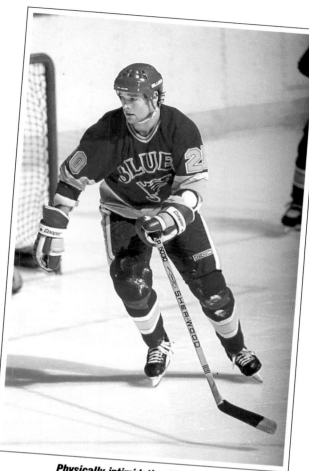

Physically intimidating Mark Hunter carries on a St. Louis tradition: hit first, ask questions later.

To bring us into hockey's modern era — a time when every team housed someone who commonly became known as the enforcer — simply look at the expansion teams of the **St. Louis Blues and the Philadelphia Flyers**.

Now the Flyers have been vilified for creating pandemonium in the NHL and for legitimising violence as a means to the Stanley Cup championship. But history shows that they were victims before they were bullies.

Both the Flyers and the Blues were charter members of the NHL's 1967 expansion. While Philadelphia stocked up on artists, the Blues went looking for musclemen.

With the help of Bob and Barclay Plager (brothers who had once fought each other on the ice, off the ice, under the stands and in the dressing rooms in a *junior* game) and Noel Picard, the Blues manhandled the Flyers for two straight seasons.

"It bothered me that we were being outhit," said Flyer owner Ed Snider. "I knew we had to do something about it."

And do it they did. If ever there was a core of players that more willingly harkened to the advice of the legendary Conn Smythe, the man who created the Maple Leafs (said Smythe, "If you can't beat 'em in the alley, you won't beat 'em on the ice") the NHL must have struck their names from all the record books.

Philadelphia's Broad Street Bullies captured two consecutive Stanley Cups during the mid-1970s and while there were always fine players on those squads, it was the bully tactics that gained all the attention.

Players like Bob "Mad Dog" Kelly, Don Saleski and Puck's ultimate bad boy, Dave Schultz, were the villains. En route to their Stanley Cups, the Flyers beat up anyone who got in their way, creating rivals just looking to catch Philadelphia asleep.

Philadelphia's Dave Poulin was just a youngster when the Blues and the Flyers were waging their ice wars.

Not all rivalries are built on violence, though the revenge factor certainly makes a great seed. One of sports' great rivalries (and some have called it the greatest) is that between the **New York Rangers and the New York Islanders**.

Born in 1972, the Islanders surfaced at a time when the Rangers were regularly challenging for the Stanley Cup. In 1975, however, the Islanders had knocked the Rangers out of the playoffs and were most certainly headed for more greatness than the Big Apple boys ever envisioned.

But in 1979, with the Islanders clearly the top team in the NHL, the Rangers pulled off a shocker of an upset in the playoffs, a back-handed "there, we're even," in a series that captured the imagination of the entire city.

"There were times during that season that I thought about playing the Islanders in the playoffs, but I always thought it would be early," recalls Anders Hedberg, now in management with the Rangers. "But to have played them in the semifinals, where it meant either us or them going to the Stanley Cup finals — that was a dream."

If any fuel was needed for this April fire, as if the playoff revenge factor wasn't enough, the Rangers' Ulf Nilsson had suffered a broken ankle in February courtesy of a check from the Islanders' Denis Potvin. Madison Square Garden's fans were simply wild over the prospect of the Islanders getting their just desserts.

With the groundwork laid — the Islanders had the best regular season record in the NHL; the Rangers had finished an improved season under first-year coach Fred Shero — the series got underway with the Rangers as the underdogs.

They pays their dues and takes their choice. Islander fans show any doubters who their favourites are.

It's been called the greatest rivalry in sports. Here, Kelly Hrudey and Ken Morrow of the New York Islanders combine to thwart the Rangers' Tomas Sandstrom.

"There were two reasons why we won that thing," Ranger goaltender John Davidson, now an analyst with "Hockey Night in Canada," remembers. "One, we were capable and two, we weren't supposed to."

Three reasons, actually, and the third was Davidson himself. Not since 1979 has a goaltender so completely carried a team, even though the Rangers had set a record for most goals scored in a series in the quarter-final set against the Flyers.

"Let's face it," says Islander forward Bob Bourne. "We were scared to death of losing to the Rangers."

But against a Madison Square Garden backdrop of 17,500 screaming faithful, while ticket scalpers sold ducats for $500 apiece, the Islanders did lose to the Rangers in six games and the dejection felt by the Long Island contingent was acute.

Potvin, crumpled on the ice after the Rangers captured the series, was in tears. Mike Bossy and Bryan Trottier had been neutralized. The Rangers had won the battle for New York.

Of course, the Islanders would later go on to win the war, gaining four straight Stanley Cup victories, stepping over the Rangers twice to get to the silverware. For the Islanders, many of whom referred to the Rangers' fans as animals ("I hate the Rangers' fans," said Bourne. "I like beating the Rangers, but I like beating their fans even more"), theirs was the last laugh.

Geography makes for good rivalries, too. There is no finer example of that than the state of war that exists between the **Montreal Canadiens and the Quebec Nordiques**.

Culture too has something to do with this one, as Canada's two primarily French-Canadian cities face off for hockey glory. But behind this rivalry there is also some corporate intrigue.

The Canadiens and Nordiques are owned by rival beer breweries (the Canadiens by Molson and the Nordiques by Carling O'Keefe), and the beer wars carry over onto the ice.

"I can think of 19 other teams I'd rather lose to," says Montreal's Larry Robinson. In fact, after the Canadiens were eliminated from the 1982 Stanley Cup playoffs by the Nords, Robinson said, "I couldn't sleep at all after we lost. I finally got out of bed at about 3 A.M. and started playing with a video game I have, one of those car things. Every time the car crashed, I hoped I was in it."

French-Canadian chauvinism is a key too. "If it comes down to a choice between a French-speaking player and an English-speaking player of the same relative talent, we're going to go with the French-speaking player," says Nordiques general manager Maurice Filion. "He'll be the player our fans most easily identify with."

And did we say beer and boardrooms? Let's not forget that Ronald Corey, president of the Canadiens, was an executive and director of O'Keefe and the Nords before he was hired by Molson. The story of Corey's appointment went on for seven pages in the next day's newspaper. In the sports section.

Reporting like that is commonplace for *La Belle Province*, where the newspapers frequently refer to the Canadiens–Nordiques feud as a civil war. Perhaps the rivalry is just that, going back to the time when the Canadiens bought an entire Quebec junior league just to acquire Jean Beliveau. Guy Lafleur is part of the lore too, signing with the Canadiens rather than the Nordiques (then of the World Hockey Association) in the early 1970s.

Beliveau had played for the Quebec Aces and Lafleur for the Remparts before making the decision to go to the Big City.

"There are many stories like that," says Mario Tremblay of the Canadiens. "Montreal loves to beat Quebec and Quebec loves to beat Montreal. Quebec fans never forget either.

"Once, while I was playing for the Montreal Juniors, we came to Quebec to play the Remparts. Well, when we skated out onto the ice the crowd booed us so hard that I asked a teammate what the hell was happening. What he said to me was: 'Don't you know? Beliveau left the Aces to play for Montreal.'"

No less bitter has been the rivalry between the Quebec Nordiques and the Montreal Canadiens. Here, Montreal captain Bob Gainey gets a leg up on former Nordiques Mario Marois.

When the Canadiens and Nordiques meet, it is a clash of old versus new, the establishment versus the upstarts. They wage war on the ice, in the boardroom and through the media. Dale Hunter and former Nordique Dan Bouchard team to stop Montreal's Mats Naslund from winning another round of the war.

As the Stanley Cup champions, the **Edmonton Oilers** probably enjoy the biggest rivalry: that of 20 other teams that want what the Oilers have, namely the Stanley Cup.

But there are two teams that Edmonton engages with more than the usual venom: the **Calgary Flames** and the **New York Islanders**.

In the Flames' case, it's a matter of geography again. The Oilers and the Flames share the province of Alberta, so factionalism plays a part in the rivalry. But, just as in any other good rivalry, one team has to take a licking from the other and the Flames do that well.

The Oilers have man-handled the Flames since the latter's arrival from Atlanta, allowing Edmonton's Andy Moog to quip: "If the games were close, there would be a real rivalry here."

But in the Smythe Division playoffs during Edmonton's first run for the Cup the Flames stretched the Oilers through a seven-game set before falling. Performances like that almost guarantee that more heartfelt battles for Alberta will be engaged.

As for the Islanders, let's say it's a case of young versus old, established champions versus the new kids on the block. To say nothing about how the Islanders bristled everytime someone mentioned Edmonton as the team of the future, especially while the Islanders still held the Cup.

So, while the rest of the NHL was writing their obituaries during the spring of 1983, and while the Oilers were obviously reading their press clippings, the Islanders simply played hockey.

Everyone was gunning for the Edmonton Oilers during their two-year Stanley Cup reign and, in the spring of 1985, may believed that Ron Sutter and the Philadelphia Flyers would upset the Oilers. But, just as he stopped Sutter here, Grant Fuhr repulsed all assaults.

The result of the final series between the two teams was a licking indeed, a true humbling of the Oilers by the still great — and still champion — Islanders. The New Yorkers swept the Oilers out of the finals and embarrassed Wayne Gretzky, holding The Great One to precisely no goals in the series. The signs posted by the fans at the Nassau Coilseum read, "Wayne Who?"

There, snickered the Islanders, we learned 'em. But it was only a year later that the two teams met again, and this time the Oilers spat in the Islanders' collective eye.

Have Bryan Trottier? asked Edmonton of New York. Well, we've got Mark Messier. No, said the Oilers, we won't trade Jari Kurri for Mike Bossy. And who's Billy Smith, anyway? He can't be as good as Grant Fuhr and Andy Moog.

Edmonton's response to their own humiliation was to administer a beating to the Islanders. Perhaps the Oilers victory was more cruel than the one they had absorbed a year prior — more cruel because it was less complete, allowing room for second-guessing and lots of what ifs.

After their loss in 1983 Edmonton could put forth no excuses, so complete was the drubbing they absorbed ("The best game we ever lost," said Gretzky after the Islanders blanked the Oilers 2–0 in the series opener that year). But the Islanders had room for excuses in 1984, and even after the loss refused to admit the better team had won.

That's the pride that make champions. That's the emotion that makes rivalries.

The Oilers fans know it is better to light just one little candle than to stumble in the dark.

NHL Gallery

Chicago's Keith Brown explains the facts of life to Minnesota's Brian Bellows . . . and don't let it happen again!

Former Buffalo winger Sean McKenna plays leapfrog with the Islanders' Denis Potvin.

A Sabres victory dance.

Pittsburgh's Mario Lemieux takes a break from
carrying the Penguins on his shoulders.

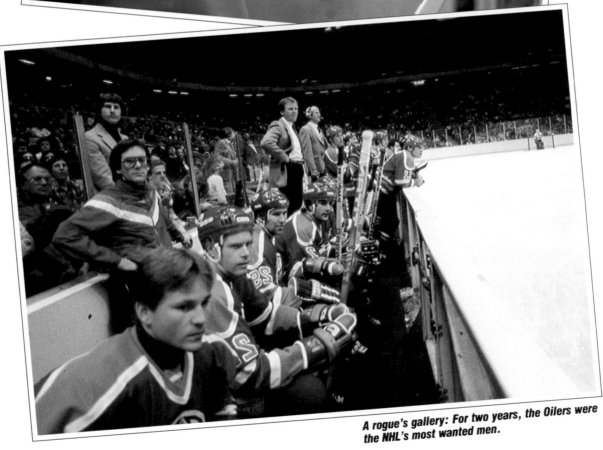

A rogue's gallery: For two years, the Oilers were
the NHL's most wanted men.

One guess what Perry Anderson has just done.

See, hockey is a game where fans can play too.

The Hartford Whalers and Montreal Canadiens search for a lost contact lens. Referee Andy Van Hellemond suggests a possible location.

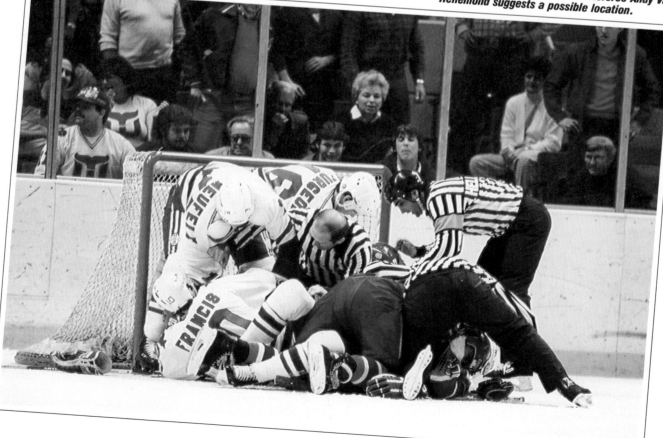

Brotherly love, Cain and Abel style: New York's Brent Sutter smites younger brother Rich.

Where have we seen this before? Montreal's Bob Gainey, Larry Robinson and Mats Naslund celebrate the win that made the Canadiens the sporting world's most successful franchise.

Calgary's John Tonelli proves to Montreal's Mike Lalor that it takes two to tango, even during the Stanley Cup finals . . .

. . . while Montreal's Chris Chelios and Calgary's Dan Quinn do the two-step.

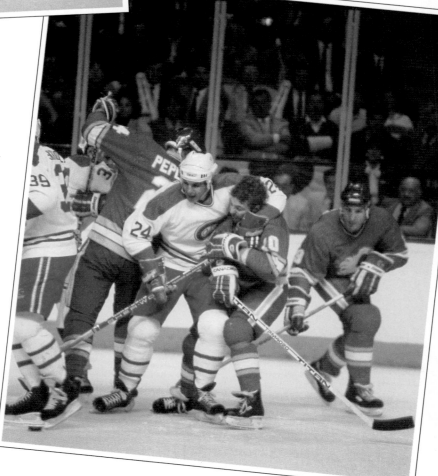

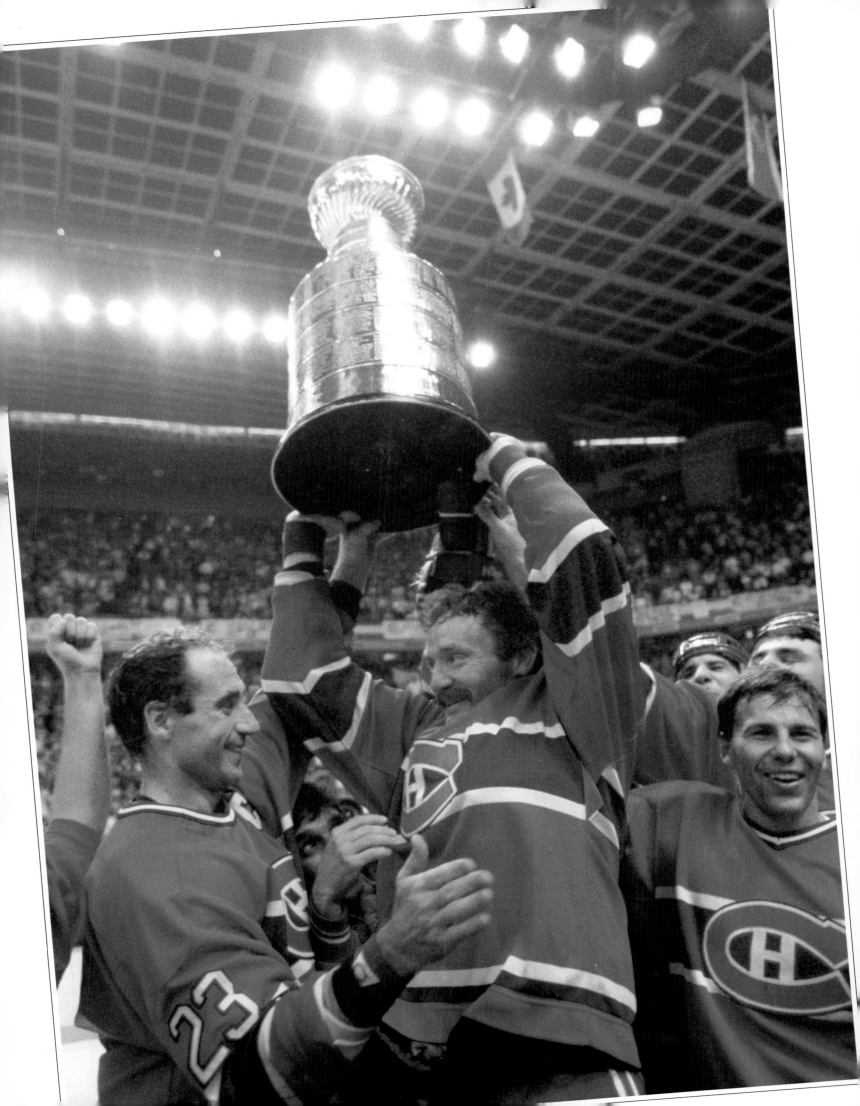

Index